T—

for your
vote of Confidence.
Norman will come around.
Peace,
Mary
314-229-1843

UGT2BLV

How God Worked In My Life

By Mary Rachelski

Copyright © 2018 by Mary I. Rachelski

All rights reserved. No part of this publication may be reproduced without the prior written permission of the author.

To protect the privacy of those who have shared their stories with the author, some names have been changed.

Cover art and photograph original design by Andy Rachelski.

All proceeds from the sale of this book will be donated by the author to the National Center on Sexual Exploitation. Learn more about them on their website - endsexualexploitation.org.

Published by Lulu.com
Printed in the United States of America

ISBN 978-0-359-21587-4

**Dedicated to Andy—
my incredible husband,
without whom I couldn't
have done any of this!**

Table of Contents

Foreword xv
Acknowledgement xix
Life After Death 1-158
How This Book Came About 3
How I Came About – 1940 6
You're Bad! – 1945 10
Aren't I Special – 1944-1950 13
Sunday's Coming – 1945-1949 15
The Twins – 1949 17
Life Changes – 1950 19
The Nun From Hell – 1950 21
It Continued – 1950+ 26
Oh Happy Day – 1952 28
My Teen Years – High School – 1956-1959 30
The Mid-1950's 33
Prayers Really Do Work! – 1959 34
For I Know What Plans I Have For You – 1962 37
Married – 1964 39
God Bless This Priest – 1968 41
Time To Move – 1973 44
Encounter With The Elderly – 1976 47
Things Are Looking Up – Inspiration To Change – 1978 52

The Biggest Mistake Of My Life – 1982 54
The Greatest Gift – 1983 58
Marriage Encounter Weekend – Fall 1984 62
Andy Hits Bottom – August 17, 1985 64
When The Student Is Ready, The Teacher Will Come
    (Recovery Sneaks Up On Me) – 1987 68
Mini-Community – 1988 72
He Proposes – 1989 77
How We Got Into Prison – 1989 80
We Just Kept Going Back To Prison – 1990-1994 82
How I Met Sue McClure – 1991 85
"THE" Break-Through Talk – 1992 91
Touched By An Angel? – 1993 94
I'm Home – We Became V.I.C.'s – 1994 99
Look Out World, Here I Come . . . To Prison – 1994-2003 102
How To Keep Love Alive 108
The Life Adventure Continues –
    A Promise Is A Promise – Spring 2001 119
We Meet A Spiritual Mentor – Fall 2001 125
Hold Onto Your Hat! – 2003 129
The Locksmith – 2005 134
Medjugorje – 2005 141
ACTS Forgiveness Talk – 2005 148
I'm The Director? – 2009 151
Help's On The Way – 2009 154

Retired – December 31, 2011	156
What I've Learned In Prison	158
Boys I Met Along The Way	**159-198**
Boys I Met Along The Way	161
Sammy	163
Robert	176
Charles	177
Ted	180
My Little Buddy – Danny	183
God's Grace – Keith	185
Drew	186
Orlando	187
Randy	188
Impress Me! – Ron	189
Good Works In Mysterious Ways – Richard	193
Walt	197
DOC Puts The "Fun" In Dysfunctional	**199-213**
Prison Worker Perspective	201
Department Of Corrections VS Delancey Street Foundation	
How Delancey Got Started	205
We Saw For Ourselves – 2002	206
How Are You Funded?	210
Epilogue	**215-224**
I Can't Remember – 2016 Until Now	217
You've Got To Believe	223

Foreword

The concept for this book came to me some time back—years back, as a matter fact. And now that the dream is finally coming to fruition, it is almost overwhelming.

The sections of this book all build, one on the other. The first one, **Life After Death**, is about my spiritual journey—from birth, through my very early childhood, to how I came to end up in prison.

If it weren't for the incredible man (my little God with skin on—Andy) that the Big God gave me to share this amazing journey; my belief in the Big God; my understanding of what I learned while growing up; the healing I received that has made me stronger—none of this would have happened. Or at least I wouldn't have recognized it as God acting in my life!

The second section**, Boys I Met Along The Way**, is about how I ended up in prison and the stories of some of the men I met there. Their impact on me and (hopefully) mine on them will give you a perspective of some of the brilliance we have locked away in our prisons today. If we could just find a way to harness that intelligence, creativity and leadership, we could heal the world.

Which brings me to the third section, **DOC Puts The "Fun" In Dysfunctional**, which is a "tongue-in-cheek" about how the Department of Corrections is so antiquated. I will be comparing it to a San Francisco operation in business now for over fifty years that has done amazing things in very short timeframes while housing both male and female "inmates" with NO STATE FUNDS.

These sections are so closely intertwined that I must constantly keep telling myself, "No, <u>this</u> story belongs in <u>that</u> section."

I hope you like reading these pages, but more than that, I hope some of what you read makes you angry. Angry enough to do something about our criminal justice system.

Now perhaps you're saying to yourselves, "Mary . . . what a strange name for a man." I am not now, nor have I ever been, a man. But yes, my stories are mostly about men I have personally met in prison.

Any and all proceeds from this book will be donated to my favorite charity, the National Center on Sexual Exploitation (NCOSE). After reading the book, you will understand why this is a cause near and dear to my heart.

Thank you, and I hope you enjoy,

Mary Rachelski

Acknowledgment

I would like to thank Vicky Meehan, an unexpected gift from God that I didn't even know I needed!

At a meeting one day, I happened to mention that I was writing a book. Weeks later, to my surprise, a women who happened to be at that meeting took me aside and told me she was an editor and that she would be honored if I would allow her to help me with my editing.

Never having written a book before, I didn't realize that I would need someone to tweak my work so that it made sense to the reader. I didn't even know what I didn't know!

To make a long story short, if it weren't for Vicky, you would not be reading this book at all. Not only did she format the book for printing, but she knew all about how to go about getting the book published. I was clueless!

When Andy and I asked Vicky how much it was going to cost to have her help us with this project, she quickly assured us, "Zero." She went on to say that God had been nudging her to make the offer from the first time she heard me talk about the book several months earlier. She found herself balking about it because of her already heavy workload. But God wouldn't let up, and she had finally come to know this was something she was being called by Him to do.

There are not enough words to thank her appropriately. Her time and energy in getting this done are colossally appreciated! And thank *you*, God, for giving her the push to do it!

Life After Death

How This Book Came About

My name is Mary Rachelski. I recently turned 78 years old. A little over a year and a half ago, I was diagnosed with early Alzheimer's. Boy, that'll get your attention! It sure got mine! At first, I felt as though I had been kicked in the stomach, by the entire football team, *with* their cleats on, *all* at the same time!

After a while, I started to look at the many gifts God has bestowed on me, and I thought, "Well, He's done a pretty good job with me thus far, and He seems to be forgiving me for all my screw-ups. I'm reasonably certain that I know where I'm going. And this whole thing is going to be tougher on my husband and family then it will be on me. Maybe Alzheimer's is not the end of the world, just the end of this world, as I know it. I'm kind of fed up with this world anyway. So, let's just go with the flow."

Now, don't let me give you the wrong idea—I'm no hero! Never have been! I'm just exasperated with the ways of this world. I'm looking forward to going to a better place. I don't want to leave my family, but that's not my call. After all, everyone is going to go someday!

So, I decided to have fun with this. Besides, it will make it easier on my loved ones. If I just sit around feeling sorry for myself, it will get to the point that they will be *glad* to see me go!

The other revelation that came to me is—I've had a good life! No, it wasn't all roses, but I have been able to get help when I needed it and have done a lot of healing. I've also been able to be there for a lot of others along the way. And, I've learned a thing or two as I went. **That, in and of itself, is worth talking about!**

I have known for some time that God has had me in the palm of His hand all along the way, even through the crappy stuff. I even had names for the sections, as you saw if you read the foreword. But I finally came to understand that I didn't really believe in myself enough to be able to do it.

Eventually, I came to realize that it is all in God's timing. After we got my diagnosis and it had time to sink in, I heard God is saying, "***NOW**, Mary,*" and He lit a fire under me! I have until tomorrow evening to hand the first draft of the first chapter in to my accountably team.

As I am not a typist, this should be interesting. I am also OCD, which means I cannot type while ignoring errors, and I *do* make errors. And I *must* correct them on the spot! Time consuming! But, I can't wait to get to the computer in the mornings. And I think about incidents that I want to be sure and remember to put in the story all through the day. Did I mention that I am lousy at keeping notes? And for those of you who are not aware, memory is one of the main problems for someone with Alzheimer's. Then I sit at the computer and try and rack my brain, what is it that was so funny that I wanted to be sure and put in here?

So, that is why you are holding this book in your hands right now. I pray that you have not just received a scary diagnosis, of any kind; but if you have, hang in here with me and let's see if I can't take your mind off your troubles for a little while.

One thing I would like to explain to you before I go too far is that you will come across the phrase, "as I came to believe or came to learn" quite often. Navigating life's path, we will come to understand things that eluded us prior to that time and moment. Sometimes it's a BFO (blinding flash of the obvious—obvious to everyone but us!). And other times, we gradually realize something that we may have seen or heard many times before, but up until that very moment, it went right over our heads unnoticed. I've learned *that* is usually when God is trying to teach us something new and/or important!

How I Came About
1940

I was born at home. That's right, at home in my parents' bed. Back in those days, children were usually born at home. I eventually became one of six offspring, but I don't want to get ahead of myself. I have been told that before they could determine my gender, I flipped over on my stomach three times. Now that tells me three things—I must have been very smart, very strong (or at least strong willed), and very demure! I was also the first girl to be born in my immediate family, at least for that generation.

I already had two older brothers—didn't receive a sister until I had been given two more brothers. Any idea what it's like growing up with four brothers? You had to constantly be on your toes. Two brothers, the one just older (Jim) and the other, just younger (Ray), were my best friends. They were there for me and helped make life easier.

Jim was my protector. Mostly from Bob, (alias Attila) our eldest brother, who was an ogre. His disposition stemmed primarily from the fact that he had Mom's backing. In her eyes, he could do no wrong. Boy, had she drunk the Kool-Aid! I wish I had a dollar for every time she asked me why couldn't I be more like Bob? What I wanted to say, was, "Well for starters, I'm a girl!" But I was too smart to open my mouth. My second thought was, "He's the last person I would want to emulate."

Ray was there to listen. When he was young, he couldn't answer back, so he did just listen. As he got older, he was passive, so he still listened, and he still does.

Life, overall, as I remember it now, was not so bad. Time has a way of dulling the pain. And I don't remember as much, because I was just a kid then.

Every year, at the start of spring, I would be affected with rheumatic fever. This repeated from the age of four until I was ten. Then I apparently out-grew it, or perhaps one of the cockamamie schemes one of the doctors came up with finally worked.

They obviously didn't know what caused it, so I became a lab rat, so to speak. They tried some nutty stuff. Moving me from tubs of scalding hot water to tubs with ice water with actual ice chips floating in it. The intent was to shock me out of it. They even bandaged my feet so tight that I couldn't walk.

My primary doctor was sweet though. Dr. Cook explained to me that my heart was like a locomotive; and if I didn't take really good care of myself and do everything I was told do, to the best if my ability, that someday that locomotive in my chest would stop running and Mary would be no more. I got the message!

I've always been open (much to my mother's chagrin) and loved talking, even to strangers. Months in bed can make one kind of stir crazy. So each year when I started to improve physically and got stronger, I was able to sit on the front steps in my pajamas and robe and watch the other kids play in front of our house.

I would talk to anyone and everyone that passed by. I was so hungry for company. People felt sorry for me because I looked pathetic—so pale from being cooped up for months. That, coupled with the fact that we were only one of about five white families in the immediate neighborhood, made me quite a novelty item.

Did I mention that my hair was glow-in-the-dark red? I hated it at the time because all the kids called me "Red," and I wasn't particularly fond of that nickname. I would be teased relentlessly by other kids (who would chant in a sing-song nasally voice that obnoxious kids have a way of doing), "I'd rather be dead then red on the head." You can only listen to that for so long before you want to hurt something! Ironically, I would love to have that color *now*. But, that's all water under the bridge.

So, as I sat on the front steps, each time someone passed by, I would barrage them with questions.

"Hi, my name is Mary, what's yours? Do you live around here? Are you married? Do you have any kids? How old are they? Do you have any pets? Where do you work?" And being polite, they would answer all my questions.

Then at dinner, I had something to talk about. I would tell the family all about my new friend Jenny, that she was married, and she and her husband had three kids and their names are . . ." I thought I was entertaining my family with all that I had learned. And, I had a very good memory, too—back then!

My family had three nicknames for me, "Babblin' Bess," "Gravlin' Gertie," and "Nosey Rosie!" At dinner I would regale the family with my gold mine of information about my new friends. And this was the thanks I got?! I was too young to realize that I was being slammed, and worse yet, my parents were the ringleaders, especially my mother. Dad was a follower.

You're Bad!
1945

"You tell me what happened! Or I'm going to call the police and tell them to come get you because *you're bad*!" My mother threatened this over seventy years ago, but I can feel it as clearly as if it happened just last week.

I was five years old. My father had recently returned from the war. Mom had gone out for the evening, and Dad was babysitting. He had put Ray, age three, to bed. That left my older brothers Jim, age nine, Bob, age eleven, and me in his charge.

"How about playing hide-and-seek?" My father always had great ideas for keeping us entertained. Mostly because we didn't have TV back then. Nobody did yet.

He was like a tall kid. The neighborhood children used to stand outside the house and summon him, "Ohhh, Mr. King, can you come out and play?" Kids didn't use doorbells in those days. Nor did they call for us as much as they called for my father. But that didn't matter; just knowing that everyone wanted to play with him made us feel special.

This night was different. This time, Dad suggested that because I was so young, I needed help hiding. We would have teams, Bob and Jim against Dad and me. "Let's play with the lights out; that will make it scarier," he suggested.

I could hear my brothers in the front part of the house counting, except that this time instead of clamping my hands over my mouth so that I wouldn't giggle and give our hiding place away, I couldn't wait for them to find us. Something was very wrong. And, I was NOT having fun!

I don't remember much of the specifics or how long it went on. However my brothers must have heard me whimpering and told Mom when she came home.

The next thing I remember, was my mother glaring at me as she held the telephone receiver against her ear while hissing through clinched teeth, "You tell me what happened! Or I'm going to call the police and tell them to come get you because *you're bad*!"

I don't even remember how that scenario played out. All I remember is her reaction to the news. The subject was never broached again. It was as if it had never happened. I would like to say that was the only time my father molested me, but it continued until I was old enough to leave home.

From that point, my mother stopped loving me, or so it felt. The only time I remember getting positive feedback was when I would eavesdrop on her phone conversations. I heard things like, "Mary is my right-hand man, I don't know what I would do without her."

To my face I heard things like, "For Christ sake, Mary, put down the God-damned doll and help me fix dinner." Nothing I did ever seemed to please her.

Aren't I Special
1944–1950

The only time I felt part of the family was during the long months of each spring when I was bed-ridden with rheumatic fever. This happened every year from the time I was four until I out-grew it at about the age of ten. It was also the only time *he* left me alone.

One side effect from the rheumatic fever I think you might find interesting is this. Like most children, I slept in the fetal position. I still do! Not good with rheumatic fever, it causes incredible joint pain, swelling and stiffness. But you're not responsible for what you do while you're asleep, right?

Each morning when I awoke, I could not straighten my legs or arms. So my mother would have to come and pull one arm out straight, in order for me to hold onto the headboard. Then she pulled the other one out, and I grabbed the headboard with both hands. She then straightened my legs, one at a time. It was incredibly painful, and the neighbors would come running to see if I was being murdered, until they got used to the noise. I often wondered if my mother was enjoying herself while doing this procedure.

Fortunately, when I was ten, someone came up with the idea to pull my back teeth. That was the last year. The rheumatic fever never returned.

Sunday's Coming
1945–1949

    Every Sunday, our family routine was to go visit the maternal grandparents who lived at the other end of town. Dinner always consisted of cold-cut sandwiches and a bakery-bought cake for dessert. It never changed.

    Grandma was in poor health. She and Mom would sit in my grandparents' bedroom and talk. On days, when the weather was bad, we had to sit on a chair and listen to them. We couldn't play in the backyard much because the noise annoyed my grandmother. On rare occasions, if the weather was nice, we would be allowed to go to the neighborhood movie theatre for a double feature. But that didn't happen until we were older. We always prayed for good weather. We were each given a quarter. It cost a dime each to get in, and then we could eat ourselves into a coma with the leftover fifteen cents. It was much cheaper to live in those days.

    On a good day, I could visit with my Aunt Mary. She was Mom's younger, unmarried sister who lived with my grandparents; and her bedroom was in the front part of the house. That was the highlight of my week. She made me feel important. We would talk while she was getting ready for an evening date. I remember her standing inside her closet with the door open. I couldn't see her, which gave her some privacy, but I didn't feel shut out. I adored Aunt Mary and always wanted to be just like her.

The Twins
1949

When I was nine, the twins were born, expanding our family by two more. A boy and a girl in that order. From then on, my sister became my mother's "little girl." Believe it or not, it wasn't that big a deal for me because I didn't really feel like I belonged there anyway.

At first, I was excited! The babies were wonderful in the beginning, and I thought of them as mine! But as they grew older and the novelty wore off, they became much more a pain. My mother assigned me the position of full-time babysitter. I would no sooner get the second one to sleep when the first one would wake up. It seemed I never got to go outside and play once I finally physically improved from the rheumatic fever because by then, the twins took precedent.

Somehow, I found a copy of my birth certificate and became convinced that I was adopted and didn't belong there. I wasn't sure why these people wouldn't believe me. It was clearly evident to me that they really didn't want me. Under birthdate, April 1 had been written, then someone crossed it out and wrote March 31, which is what I have always known my birthday to be. It also stated that I was one of triplets, but then that, too, was crossed out and "single birth" was written in. I vaguely remember hearing a long time ago that the doctor who delivered me was known to have a bit of a drinking problem. I do know that he also delivered my mother, so that meant that he must have been pretty old.

Anyway, I now had three children to look after—Ray and the twins. Ultimately, I grew to hate those twins. As soon as I went outside to play, I'd hear Mom calling, "Mary, the twins are up." What did I care? I didn't have those kids, why did I have to be the one to take care of them? *She* was their mother.

Life Changes
1950

One Sunday evening as we were having dinner at Grandma's, Aunt Mary's boyfriend, Norm (later to become *Uncle* Norm), asked, "So, what do you kids think of the idea of having to go to a school with "Kraut nuns?" All conversation came to a screeching halt. You could almost hear the mice in the walls picking their teeth.

Our maternal grandmother had recently suffered another stroke, and Grandpa needed help with her care. That's when we learned we were being pulled from our school and moved across town to live above our grandparents. That meant we would have to change schools. The nuns at St. Agnes (which was to be our new school) were all from Germany, and they spoke with pronounced accents.

As usual, I was the first to break the silence. "What's a Kraut nun?" The only answer I received was, "You'll find out!"

Because of the move, I would have to leave three women that meant the world to me—Mrs. Carpenter (my *chosen* "surrogate-grandmother") and her daughter, and Sister Angelica.

The Carpenters ran the re-sale store next to our house and would always bring me like-new dolls and coloring books to keep me entertained, especially when I was bedridden.

Sister Angelica was my current fourth-grade teacher at St. Theresa's, and she looked (and acted) just like her name. We had never had another nun pull up her long black skirt and tuck it into the Rosary beads that hung from her waist so that she could run and play with us.

I asked Sister Angelica about St. Agnes, and she told me the school was run by nuns that were all born in Germany. She advised me that the term "Kraut" was a rude title used when referring to people from Germany.

I would be leaving my beloved Sister Angelica. If there was a God, why was He doing this? I was devastated to have to move, but a few months before school would let out for the summer, we were transferred to St. Agnes at the other end of the city. They couldn't even let us complete the school year!

Up until now, all the nuns at St. Theresa's school felt sorry for me and had automatically promoted me to the next grade, despite the large number of days absent due to illness. The prospect of what was to come was terrifying.

The Nun from Hell
1950

The first words I heard from the welcoming committee of one sounded like they came from a jaw that was locked from the inside. "Kraut nuns, huh? Well, we'll see about *that* won't we, missy!" Leaning over me was a very red face. Protruding from a white cardboard frame and black veil was something looking much like pink bread dough being pushed out of a tube. Wire-rimmed glasses were the only thing keeping the eyes from popping out of the head. Meet Sister Carmeana, my *new* fourth-grade teacher.

It wasn't long before I learned why the kids called her Sister <u>Car-meean</u>-na behind her back. The entire school population, even upperclassmen, feared her! She would have the eighth-grade boys down on their knees in the school yard, begging for mercy. She liked to dig her nails into the soft underside of the upper arm and rub the nerves back and forth across the bone. Students were known to routinely confess to things they hadn't done, just to get her to stop.

I made the mistake of showing my mother the marks on my underarm the first time I was inflicted. It was lunch hour. Mom grabbed me and half-drug me over to the priest house to show the pastor. Not only did I miss lunch, but guess who was waiting for me when I got back to school that day. I was greeted with the comment, "Well, snitch, you're going to regret *that* little move."

She walked with a pronounced limp, pronounced because you heard her coming long before she arrived. One leg was shorter than the other, and she walked with this rhythmic pattern, made by the combination of the shortness of the leg and the rosary beads jingling from her waist. It sounded kind of like this: thump-thump, chink-chink, thump-thump, chink-chink. Our being able to hear her coming only added to her frustration, as it made it more difficult for her to catch us at as much wrongdoing as she would have liked. The rumor was that she had undergone eighteen surgeries in one year—probably a slight exaggeration, but still, it might explain a lot.

It was very evident that she disliked children. Well, all but two. A girl named Jane and a boy named John were her favorites. The rest of us were referred to as "morons."

When we read out loud to the class, we would have to stand next to her at her desk while she moved a pencil under the words. She moved very quickly! And if we made a mistake, she would rap our knuckles with the metal strip of the ruler. My knuckles are still callused; as I'm sure are a lot of my former classmates'.

She also had a paddle from a ball-and-paddle kid's toy. She had removed the ball and rubber band and painted the paddle bright red. She was *not* afraid to use it. Remember, these were the days *long before* child abuse could get you jail time.

One day I had done something to really upset her. I don't remember what it was; it didn't take much. I've probably blocked it from my subconscious. Sister brought me up to the front of the class, made me lie across the desk, **pulled my skirt up over my head** and preceded to paddle me in front of the entire class. *Boys* and girls! I was not going to give her the satisfaction of making me cry, so I prayed, and I prayed, and I prayed. God was with me that day because He helped me to remain stubborn enough not to cry. But that only fueled the fire.

One Saturday, I was out walking the twins in their double-stroller. When I got to the end of the block, to my surprise I was standing in front of a classmate's house. I said, "Hi Melissa. How are you?" and her answer was, "Why don't you go back where you came from; you're not wanted here." I was royally crushed! But I was not going to show her that her comment hurt. So, I turned on my heal and walked the other way without looking back.

Less than a week later, Sister Carmeana sent me to the blackboard to do a math problem. Now math was not then, nor is it now, my strong suit. I struggled with the problem. Finally, Sister asked someone to come to the board and help me. I was incredibly relieved, until I realized that she had sent Melissa. Sister's parting words were, "And Melissa, if she makes a mistake, give her a shove."

Well I did make a mistake, and Melissa shoved me. I made another one; she shoved me again. On the third mistake she had this evil look in her eye, like she was really enjoying herself. I don't know if it was the look, pure meanness on my part, if it was the remark that Saturday while I was walking the twins—it could even have been the paddling in front of the entire class weeks before—but I lost it! When she shoved me for the third time, I shoved her right back. And knocked her flat on her butt!

I don't remember what happened after that, I guess I blacked out. All I heard was thump-thump, chink-chink, thump-thump, chink-chink. I was told she pulled out all the stops. The underarm dig, the paddling, even pulled my hair and slapped me a few times. At least this is what I heard. My memory of the physical pain of this ordeal (thankfully!) has been numbed by my brain.

Because we had transferred in the middle of the year and I had missed so much school at St. Theresa's (due to the rheumatic fever), both of my favorite brothers and I were held back for another full year.

How could I possibly be doomed to another full year with this monster?!

As a result of these experiences, when I became an adult, I spent many hours in a therapist's office. My therapist had me write this story as a college project and part of my therapy. Thanks to her, my recovery time on this issue was relatively short, because by the time I finished writing the story, God and my therapist had helped me see the whole thing differently. What could have turned out to be a story of tragedy became a story of comedy. I was able to let it go and forgive her, although posthumously. AND, I got an "A" from my therapist!

It Continued
1950+

Now I had two more perpetrators, my grandfather and Sister Carmeana, (pronounced Car-***mean***-na).

She didn't *sexually* abuse me, but she lived up to her name. Sister made my life miserable during the day, and Dad did the same most nights. And with my grandfather living downstairs, there weren't many safe places around.

I was not well-liked growing up. I was homely. I was usually dirty. Cleanliness was not high on my list of priorities. It wasn't safe to be caught nude in the tub, in a bathroom with no lock on the door. All my life I had the sensation of being "odd man out." I always felt as if I had my nose pressed up against the glass. I was so lonely. My younger brother, Ray (two years my junior) was everything to me. I think he was the only thing that kept me sane all the way through high school.

Sister would humiliate me in front of class, and I couldn't even come home and tell my mother what she had done without her accusing, "Well what did *you* do to make her mad?" On some level, I think that's why, as I grew older, I made it easy for my father and grandfather. In some sick way, they were showing me love. And I equated sex with love.

Oh, Happy Day!
1952

I often wondered how my mother could not know what was going on with my father and grandfather. So often I would beg her not to go out, or at least to take me with her; but my pleas always fell on deaf ears. Then one year when I was about twelve or thirteen, she handed me a beautifully wrapped birthday gift two weeks early. This was very strange because birthdays usually went by almost as an afterthought. My instructions were to not open it, not even shake it until my birthday. So, for two weeks, my imagination ran wild.

On the big day, I was nearly breathless while opening the box. I was so excited! She stood there the whole time, watching me open it and waiting for my reaction. Imagine my confusion to find two pair of nylon, ***see-through*** pajamas!

Four decades later while sharing this story with my therapist, to my amazement, she quietly said, "She set you up!"

"What?!" I asked.

"Didn't you tell me that your father was very open about the fact that your mother didn't like sex? Didn't she, herself, tell you repeatedly, that all men had only one thing on their minds? Didn't she tell you that she thought of sex as her *duty* as a Catholic?"

My answer was, "Yes" to all three questions. How could I have been so blind?

Another aspect of this pajama event was that when I grew up, married and had children, I hated receiving gifts, and they hated giving me gifts, because my reaction was always anti-climactic. I always had trouble hiding my disappointment, even if I *had* no expectations as to what I was going to receive. I never even made that connection until just now writing this . . . God moves in mysterious ways!

My Teen Years
High School
1956–1959

I had trouble making friends in high school because I was never in one school very long. I started my freshman year in 1956 at Hadley in north St. Louis because I had a part time job at a theatre near Hadley. It was a technical school. We received credits from our employer as well as our teachers—quite progressive at the time.

The next year, in 1957, another NEW technical school opened named O'Fallon. All the students who lived in south St. Louis were transferred from Hadley to O'Fallon.

During the summer of 1958, I transferred to McKinley as it was closer to home, and we could walk to and from school. I was also told I had to go to summer school because I wasn't going to have enough credits to graduate in 1959 if I didn't. So, I spent the summer at Roosevelt High School gathering credits.

In the fall of 1958, I found out that someone in the office had miscalculated, and I would have *more* than enough credits to graduate. So, I finished my academic endeavors at McKinley, which was within walking distance from home. Also, my younger brother, Ray was a freshman now, so we walked together—a benefit I enjoyed enormously. The down side of this daily walk together was that everyone thought we were going steady.

It didn't take me long to adopt a new partner in crime at McKinley. I met Leon Taylor, fellow student, and we hit it off from the start—so well as a matter-of-fact that we both ended up in the principal's office on the third day of school.

He was new and different! Leon lived life large. He didn't walk, he *danced* down the halls, while singing, "Peanuts! Oh, oh, oh, oh, oh, oh, Peanuts!" He reminded me of my old neighborhood because Leon was African-American. And I missed the closeness people of color always seemed to hold for each other. In my opinion, whites never shared the same kind of bond.

Leon and I were in an art class together, and he backed me when the instructor tried to tell us that we become zombies when we shop in the grocery stores. He contended the shelves are stocked to grab our attention, so that we will put things into our carts that we don't even use or need but take anyway because of the way the stores are set up. I argued, "If I was on a budget, I would be more cognizant of my purchases." Leon took my side, and the teacher took offense. Hence our trip to the principal's office. Lucky for us, the principal took our side as well. Which didn't endear us or earn any bonus points with the art instructor at all.

Years later, I read somewhere that stores *are* exactly set up in this way even today! So, my advice here is—be very aware of your purchases, make a list! And follow it!

Later, I took Leon's side when he was not invited to the class reunion, and I refused to go. If Leon wasn't good enough to be invited, then neither was I. I never went to any of my class reunions.

I've often wondered whatever happened to Leon Taylor, class of 1959 at McKinley High School, St. Louis, Missouri. If you ever run into him, I would love to hear from him, or you.

The Mid-1950's

As a young woman, I became very promiscuous. And there were consequences to that promiscuity. Not uncommon for someone coming from sexual abuse. It's either that, or the victims themselves become pedophiles. Fortunately for me, drugs weren't as popular back then, and I really didn't care for the taste of alcohol; nor did I like the feeling of dizziness it caused.

But, I still had this craving for love. Or, what I thought was love. Fortunately, too, God does for us what we cannot do for ourselves. He sent me someone I had been praying for since I was a little girl. I just didn't know his name. I remember asking God to send me someone who would love, honor and cherish me. At that time, I probably didn't even know what the word "cherish" meant.

Prayers Really Do Work!
1959

Shortly after I graduated high school in 1959, I met Leo. He was one of a group of guys and gals that all hung out at the "Right Way" Diner, on the corner of Jefferson and Gravois in south St. Louis city. I was never sure why the manager let us sit there all evening, *every* evening, nursing cokes and sharing fries. We certainly were not making him rich. I think he just liked the energy, and he knew that if we were there, we were not out tearing up the neighborhood. We were fun-loving, but not rowdy. Maybe he didn't like being there by himself. But almost any night of the week, you would find the better part of approximately thirty teenagers occupying space there, talking and laughing like they didn't have a care in the world.

Leo and I had a comfortable relationship, except I found out later he liked to "play the field," and I have always been a "one-man-woman." Once we went to a last-minute Halloween party we heard about. Another friend, Leo and I went home to change before crashing the party. When they picked me up, I was dressed as a clown, and they had simply changed to fresher shirts. I felt like a *clown,* too, when I saw they weren't in costume.

Later that evening, I went to the bathroom and found Leo and another girl making out! I was crushed! We continued to date, on and off, for a couple more years, but I could never really trust him after that. He was a good guy—he just had this one small fetish. And it fueled my feeling of not ever being quite good enough!

Then one Saturday morning, I received a phone call from a girlfriend screaming into the phone, "Turn on the radio!" I flipped it on just as they were giving the news. They were talking about this young eighteen-year-old boy that was killed in an auto accident the night before.

My first thought was, *what does this have to do with me*? My Leo was twenty-one—old enough to vote, and he was very excited about the prospect of that happening.

But it *was* my Leo. They just got his age wrong. Some strange girl had shown up at the burger shop where we practically lived. She asked Leo for a ride home. He, being a good guy, said, "Sure."

Leo had a beautiful 1958 emerald-green Chevrolet convertible in which he took great pride. It was his most prized possession. While turning onto her street, a drunk driver hit him from the rear, sending Leo through the roof of the car and straight into a telephone poll. He never knew what hit him.

The mystery girl, on the other hand, sustained a sprained ankle. We later learned at the funeral that this was the third accident she had been involved in where the driver was killed. Afterwards, none of us ever saw her again.

In spite of everything I'd been through, I have never experienced pain like that in my life! Even breathing seemed impossible. I thought life was over for *me*, too. And I was glad, because I felt like I wanted to die. All I could do was lay on the living room sofa and just wail. My mother stayed in the kitchen because she didn't know what to do with me. I had read once that the Holy Spirit can understand our wailing through pain. That thought is what kept me sane.

For I Know What Plans I Have For You
1962

My knight-in-shining-armor appeared in October, 1962, and his name was Andy. And his job was to help me heal.

I met him on a job interview. He was to be my new boss. We had to set up the electronics department in a new discount store opening in my town. He was from Michigan. We worked together closely, preparing for the grand opening which was to happen in three days.

We worked fourteen hour shifts for three consecutive days, and when he asked me to do one small job before closing with the promise of going out for a burger afterwards, I couldn't resist.

I called my mother to let her know I would be a little late. Oddly, she instructed me to get straight home! "You've worked fourteen hours for three days in a row, and you need your rest!" Funny, she never cared about my rest before!? For the first time in my life, I spoke up for myself. I really wanted to go! She slammed the phone in my ear, and I knew I would pay for my decision. But I didn't care!

Andy and I talked for hours, never searching for something to say. It was so easy and comfortable. I invited him to Sunday Mass with me for the next morning. Much to my surprise, he accepted.

Why he ever wanted to see me again, I'll never know. My parents were at that service, and they were so rude to him, I was embarrassed for them.

Andy was like a breath of fresh air for me. He was the first guy I dated that I didn't have to fend off physically. As a matter-of-fact, I think I made the first move on him about a year later. I still believed that love involved sex. I couldn't comprehend how comfortable I felt with him. It was as if we had known each other all our lives.

Married
1964

In 1964, we were married.

I was pregnant, as I had been on two previous occasions in the past with other men. But Andy didn't leave me to clean up the mess alone, as I'd done previously. He wanted to be with me and do the right thing.

Our first son, Mark, was born that same year. We had another son, Scott, in 1965. After a miscarriage in 1966, I got pregnant again the *very* next month. Matt was born early in 1967. In 1968 when we found out I was pregnant for the fifth time in four years, I went into such a state of depression that I contemplated suicide.

I had it all planned. I was going to pile my three boys into the car, start the engine, and read to them until we all passed out from carbon monoxide poisoning. I was so serious that Andy was afraid to go to work. He wasn't sure what he would find when he returned. Fortunately for all of us, we only had a carport; and my husband was astute enough to tell me my plan wouldn't work without a garage!

Even though, thanks to Andy, we had always attended Mass regularly during our marriage, I wasn't much into prayer in those days.

Unless you count foxhole prayers when life had my back against the wall for some reason. Somehow, we made it through that dark time.

I finally reached a point during the pregnancy where I turned a corner. In fact, I could hardly wait for the baby's delivery. This time, God blessed us with a beautiful daughter.

God Bless This Priest
1968

After our daughter Stacy was born, I went to confession and told the young priest at our parish how I had been suicidal and how scared I was. I didn't even want Andy to come near me anymore because every time he so much as looked at me, it seemed I became pregnant!

At that session, the priest told me, "Yes, God wanted us to propagate. You've done that quite well, and in a timely manner, too, I might add! But He doesn't want you to be so faithful that you might ruin your health and not be there for your husband and children."

So, I went home and told Andy he was going to have a bad week if he wanted to stay married to me. That's when Andy met Dr. Sunshine. I kid you not, his name was actually *Sunshine*. Andy made a decision to turn off his baby-making machine. Given our fertility record thus far, we weren't going to push our luck.

Up until this point, because our children were so close in age, we usually had at least two in diapers. Each time I went into the hospital to have another one, my mother would potty-train the last one born. When our daughter finally arrived, we breathed a huge sigh of relief. It had begun to seem like we would have toddlers around the house for the rest of our lives. I remember Andy telling me shortly after Stacy's delivery, "I was beginning to think I didn't know how to make girls, and I had the pattern right in front of me!" Gratefully, we discovered girls are easier to potty-train then boys.

During the baby boom, Andy was still traveling, opening more stores in new towns. Then he decided he needed to get his degree in order to better support us. That was a very hard time because I was well out-numbered with children who were constantly fighting. As a young and relatively new mother, I didn't understand they were just looking for attention; and negative attention was better than no attention.

By this time, I was constantly exhausted. Sleep provided escape and became my drug of choice. I would just lay on the couch in the living room and snooze. I believed I was right there if something happened, so the children were safe. They kept themselves entertained by asking me questions while I was sleeping, laughing hysterically at the silly answers they got.

Sometime after all the kids were born, my parents started coming out to our house in Crestwood on Saturday evenings. With four children ages five and under, we couldn't afford to go out much, so my parents would come by. After the little ones were all in bed, we would play cards.

My relationship with Mom had greatly improved by this time, but for the most part, she was still cool towards Andy.

One night after finally getting the kids in bed, I was relaxing on the couch talking to Mom. She excused herself to use the bathroom, and when she came back, she had a look on her face as if she had seen a ghost!

"What's wrong," I asked.

She said, "I just came down the hallway, and as I passed the kids' room, I looked in and saw Andy laying on the floor between the two sets of bunk beds. He was reading 'a bed night story' [as my kids called it] to the children."

"Yeah? So?" was my response.

"Well, any man who works full time and spends all evening going to college to better the family income, and *still* takes time to read to his children, can't be all bad!"

I don't even know if she registered my answer to her, "I've been trying to tell you that for years."

Time To Move
1973

When the children all got old enough to be in school all day, I found a job outside the home to help with the income and keep myself busy. As all four of the children were sharing one bedroom, we definitely needed more space. Two sets of bunk beds in one room weren't cutting it any more. Stacy needed her own room. The extra income I earned helped us upgrade to a larger house.

Adjusting to this new neighborhood in 1973 was a learning experience for all of us. We had only moved eight miles west. But it seemed all the families in our subdivision had two-point-five children; and anyone with four children in one household was looked down upon as white trash.

Mark, who was just turning ten when we moved, probably had the hardest time adjusting. He was the oldest, and I relied heavily on him to help me parent the other children. In addition, he was bigger than most of the other boys in the neighborhood, and the mothers didn't want him playing with their toys because they were afraid he would break them. So, Mark spent a great deal of time in his room entertaining himself.

To his credit, Mark has a beautiful voice. Many of those inordinate hours he spent in his room alone, he spent singing. And, he seemed content to do that. It wasn't until years later that we realized he must have been struggling during this time because it seemed as if his social skills suffered as he got older. Happily, he's grown into a very successful man, with honesty and integrity as his strongest traits.

Scott, our second son, also grew up to be very successful, and his integrity is above reproach. However, ever since he was young, we noticed Scott has a fairness issue that gets in the way of life at times. On the up side, he will fight FOR his clients and make sure that they get the best deal. On the down side, you don't want to play a game with him!

In a way, I wonder if I might have partially been responsible for some of this. I remember once when Scott was about nine, he asked me, "Mom, why do you always ask *me* to do things for you and not Mark or Matt?"

Without thinking, my answer was, "Because you will do it without giving me any flack." Little did I know what message I was sending him at the time.

Our third son, Matt, has a gift of being very personable and loves to communicate with people. Like his brothers, he gives one hundred and ten percent, and takes the welfare of his clients very seriously. His easy sense of humor contributes to his character and serves him well.

Our daughter Stacy was my much-needed female counterpart. She balanced things out for me with all that testosterone! As an adult, Stacy has grown to be my best girlfriend, although when she was about ten, she would call me Mrs. Rachelski when she was in front of others because she didn't want anyone to know that I was her mother. I acted like I thought it was cute at the time, but I wondered if I should be doing something differently. Fact is, she was just being a typical teenager.

As much of a struggle as moving to that new neighborhood seemed at the time, we ended up staying there for the rest of the kids' childhoods. God put us exactly where we were supposed to be, just as He's done so very many times over the course of my life. But in 1973, things sure looked different!

Encounter With The Elderly
1976

In 1976, I was lucky enough to land a job in a nursing home. I was working the graveyard shift so that we had the kids covered. Andy worked days, and I worked the eleven PM to seven AM shift. It was tough, being apart so much of the time; but when you have two parents and four small children, you must have teamwork to make ends meet.

I loved the job, and I especially enjoyed working with the older generation. So many of them are forgotten souls. The best part was getting to know each resident and being able to take the time to sit and visit with them once we had everyone bedded down for the night.

I remember one man who had a brain aneurism and was only with us for very short time. He was a little delusional. He thought he was moving and wanted me to help him write a newspaper ad to try and sell some appliances. So, I stood next to his bed with a notepad and pen, pretending I was writing while he tried to compose what he wanted to say. Then, suddenly, he screamed out, *"Oh My God! My head, my head!"* I pulled the emergency cord on his call button, but within minutes, he was gone! It sure puts you in touch with your mortality, and how quickly life slips away.

Mrs. Drew was very memorable. She was always afraid she might be bothering us by putting on her call light during the night. As I answered her light one evening, she asked if she had awakened me. "No," I told her, "I was sewing." She asked what I was sewing. I told her it was an outfit I was making for our daughter. Then she asked how many children I had. When I told her four, she said, *"Oh, my, FOUR! You must have been something else between the sheets!"*

Then there was the time Mr. Bailey needed help with the urinal, but he wanted to know if I had any experience "working with males." When I told him, I had a husband and three sons, I guess he figured I was qualified.

But my favorite patient was Mr. Kelly. I remember encountering him in the hallway one evening. He was wearing nothing but a tee-shirt, and he seemed quite confused. I asked whether he was on his way TO or FROM the bathroom. His response—"I'm not sure." As I gazed down at the floor, I replied, *"Judging from the dribbling, I'd say you were going in, and you might want to step it up!"*

Another night, I was making rounds when I heard Mr. Kelly grunting, I asked if he was okay and whether I could be of assistance. He told me he was trying to close the urinal. That's when I realized that he was still in it. So, I said, "Let's see if I can help you there, OK?" "Sure," he said. So, I pulled he urinal away from his body and then snapped the lid, asking, "How's that?" His answer was, *"Great! And it doesn't hurt as much either!"*

My last night I worked at the nursing home, for whatever reason, I was driving Andy's freshly painted school-bus-yellow Fiat Spyder to work. Andy's parting words to me were, *"I love you, and take good care of my car!"* It happened to be the evening they had just finished resurfacing the road I traveled each day to work.

Unbeknownst to me, they left an eighteen-inch drop-off from the blacktop to the side of the road. As I came up the hill and around a curve, I cut it a little too wide and my tire slipped off the edge of the blacktop. The tire locked into that position as if I were on a train rail. Careening along, I was staring directly at a huge tree that must have been six feet in diameter and was dead center of the driver's position! All I had time to do was say, "Help me Jesus!" and yank the steering wheel as hard to the left as possible! Lucky for me, it was enough so that the impact was diverted from the driver's side. But it certainly didn't save the car!

Nearby, while inside their home, a father and teenage boy heard the crash and found me wandering the road. My white nurse's uniform was covered in blood. And I was incoherent. They took me back to their house and pulled a chair into the entry foyer for me to sit on while we waited for the ambulance to arrive. All I can remember about them is that I did not want to go into the living room for fear of bleeding on their carpet.

I was very blessed to be able to walk away from that car. My injuries were mild compared to those of the automobile, which was totaled!

It seems that I took out the dashboard with my face and knees, despite the seat belt. My upper denture, which I received just three weeks prior to meeting Andy, was broken from front to back; and a front tooth was buried in my lower lip. My right elbow was raw, badly torn open from hitting the gearshift lever. And I ended up with a psychedelic stripe across my chest and stomach from the seatbelt, along with severe pain in those areas *and* my knees. But I was alive! And it could have been so much worse!

On the ride to the hospital, I must have passed out. When I came to, I was looking into a beautiful man's face whom I immediately thought was Christ, complete with beard! I asked, *"Am I dead?"* He chuckled, looking up at someone sitting behind my head in the ambulance and saying, *"I need to shave this beard!"*

My injuries prevented me from working for the next couple of weeks. The morning I returned, as I was opening a hot water bottle to empty it, I felt *and heard* something in my back pop! The sensation was as if someone had reached under my right shoulder blade and pulled it out of the socket! Apparently, my days of lifting older folks were over!

Things Are Looking Up Inspiration To Change
1978

In 1978, we went to our first motivational rally. Over the years, we've been blessed to attend several life-changing seminars. I learned that both my parents had been sexually abused, and I knew neither had sought recovery. They didn't even talk about it. In those days, everything was kept in secret—I suppose it was due to shame. I chose to break that chain by writing this book.

We've been very blessed to have meaningful life experiences and to be affiliated with people like Jack Canfield of *Chicken Soup for the Soul* fame, John Gray of *Men are from Mars* . . . and Tony Robbins. We even did the Anthony Robbins fire walk in downtown Denver. Each time we participated in one of those seminars, the experience sent me back into therapy to peal yet another layer.

From those motivational rallies, we bought (and I listened to almost non-stop) tapes from many authors. I drank that material in almost constantly. Especially Jack Canfield's material on self-esteem. Every day on my way to and from work, I would listen to *200 Affirmations*. At first, I would cry because they all sounded like lies; but after a while I would cry because I *knew* they were the truth, and my heart would swell. Especially when I got to the last one, which told me, "*My being here makes a difference.*" Because my being here DID make a difference, especially to the people with whom I was now working. And I was growing spiritually as well.

I listened to that affirmations tape for forty minutes a day—all the way to work and again all the way home—for at least a whole year. Through this practice, I learned to love and appreciate myself. I also came to understand that it's not what happens to me that defines who I am, but how I *react* to what happens that does.

The Biggest Mistake Of My Life
1982

I had gone to work at a large company in mid-downtown St. Louis. My neighbor worked in management there and was able to help me get hired. This was a God-send after I lost my nursing home job due to the injuries I had sustained from the auto accident.

The only reason I went to work in the first place was because I wanted to re-model our kitchen. I thought I would have a better time selling the idea to Andy if it didn't cost him anything, and I could pay for the renovation from my salary. Everything worked out very well. The kitchen was done and paid for (to everyone's delight) in a timely manner. Only one small hitch with my new career.

The office duties worked out beautifully for me, and I got along great with the other staff members. There were a group of five women, and we all worked well together. Even though I was new, it seemed as if we had been doing it for years. I learned the system quickly, and apparently, picked up right where the person I replaced had left off.

We all talked together as we worked, so it was kind of like a gab-fest, except we were all getting paid for working and the tasks got done. The bosses were happy. We were happy. It was a dream job come true.

I had been having trouble at home with mood swings. Things had gotten tense between Andy and me. I thought it might be because I was working full-time, and he had to pick up a little more of the slack at home.

One of the gals had suggested I see her ob-gyn when I mentioned that Andy and I weren't getting along well at home. I was even having run-ins with the children, which was completely out of character for me. Because the home situation had been going on for some time, I knew that it didn't have anything to do with the new job.

Well, I went to the new doctor, and the first thing she suggested was that we do a blood test.

The blood test came back showing my hormones were *all* out of whack. She believed it might be because of the five pregnancies so close together. She said that it sounded like I was suffering from PTSD and probably had been for at least the last ten years. My body didn't have time to recover from one pregnancy before I was pregnant again. So, she put me on hormone replacement therapy. Amazingly, within a short time, I felt like a whole new woman.

However, several down sides presented themselves. One was that I later started showing spider veins around my lower legs and ankles. Also, I still must shave (just like a man) every morning. But my family is intact, and I didn't kill anyone! That's good enough for me!

By this time, Andy and I had stopped making our marriage a priority, and our feelings for each other became strained. We had been married about fifteen years, and it was as if we had "hit the wall."

I guess I was at the office job a little over a year when a new guy came into an adjoining department. Our departments didn't actually work together, but they did overlap with one another, so we had contact.

So, when I was walking down the hall one day, and the guy I mentioned earlier was walking in the opposite direction, all he did was mouth the words, "I love you." Suddenly I was like a teenager in heat! Before I knew it, we were meeting in the stairwells and calling each other at our desks. It was crazy and dangerous, but most of all, it was wrong!

We had made plans to stay late one evening, waiting until everyone else left, and then meet. So, imagine my surprise when the phone on my desk ring and I answered it with a very cherry, *"Hello, love!"* There was a pause, then Andy's voice said, *"Is that the way you answer a business phone?*" I quickly lied and said, "*I had a feeling it was you.*" But he wasn't buying it.

So, I called the other guy and told him that I would ***not*** be there. Then I went home that evening and gave Andy a night to remember, but it was out of guilt. And I'm sure he knew it.

The next day I went in, gave my notice, and quit. We both realized how close we had come to blowing what certainly was a marriage made in heaven. The problem was, we both needed to grow up and make some serious changes. We made a conscious decision to not ever let it get that close to disaster again. Even though the affair had never officially been consummated, I have still been unable to *totally* forgive myself, in spite of the fact Andy and I have now been married fifty-five years.

The Greatest Gift
1983

In 1983, my mother, with whom I now had a reasonably good relationship, called to tell me that two men had walked in one door and out another, of their house while she and Dad had been out working in the yard. They lived on a busy corner in St. Louis city. On their way through, the men picked up her wedding band and wristwatch from the dinning-room table.

This gave my siblings and me an idea for her Christmas gift, to replace her wedding band. However, somehow, she got wind of it and insisted that she would refuse it if we went through with the idea. So, my siblings sent me to "talk some sense into her." Being a people-pleasing-co-dependent—I went. I am also a very good sales person.

After explaining to her that if she could no longer have the ring Dad had given her fifty years earlier, what better gift then one from her children? She finally agreed before leveling me with a request for which I was not prepared.

Dad had already left the room by this time. He had gone down to his basement workshop after she agreed to accept the ring.

Mom wanted me to talk to Dad regarding his lack of personal hygiene, which left *a lot* to be desired. First of all, he worked in a factory where he operated a machine, and the oil from the machine was imbedded in his skin. He never wore deodorant, nor did he floss his teeth. Bathing only happened once a week, regardless of the season. It was summer now, and she had to sleep with her head at the foot of the bed to escape the smell of his breath. She believed the smell of his feet was the lesser of the two evils.

What a day that turned out to be! I tried very hard not be alone with or make physical contact with my father. Although he never touched me inappropriately again after I left home, I still didn't feel safe being alone with him. Andy and I were also very careful to be sure that he was never left alone with any of our children for the same reason.

After explaining to him that he needed to take better care of himself, I was planning my quick escape. I started to bolt for the stairs when he said, "Wait!"

"What?" I cautiously asked.

"I need to say something to you."

"Whaaat?" I slowly asked again.

"I owe you an apology," was his reply. "The way I treated you while you were growing up . . . I had no right! You did nothing to deserve my advances." He continued on to say that he would never hurt me again. And he would sooner cut his hands off than hurt our children. To the best of my knowledge, he honored that promise and never did harm any of our kids.

I was so stunned that I had no idea how to respond. I simply fluffed it off saying, "That's okay, Dad." I was just focusing on getting out of there as fast as possible. But the odd thing was, it *WAS* okay! His apology was the most AWESOME gift I had ever received in my life. As I reflected on the conversation, I realized that my animosity had been lifted! No more shame either!

It was as if all the anger I had built up just drained right out of me, down my body, until it leaked out the soles of my feet! And at the same moment, it was as if he had apologized for my grandfather and all the boys and other men who had done me wrong in my life as well! It doesn't get any better than that!

About a year after my mother's death in 1986 from a massive coronary, my sister shared some things with me about Mom's own incest experience that I never knew before. It was then that I recognized how angry I still was with her. In all those years, she did nothing to protect me from either man. As a matter-of-fact, she blamed me! If she had just told me about her past, I wouldn't have felt so all alone and dirty!

Forgiving someone who is trying to make amends is one thing. Dealing with anger for someone who is already gone (and has never shown the slightest remorse) is much more of a challenge. It took me the better part of fifteen years to work through that anger. And sometimes, it can still rear its ugly head.

Marriage Encounter Weekend
Fall 1984

In the autumn of 1984, we were asked to go on a church-sponsored *Marriage Encounter* weekend as a renewal of our wedding vows, Andy was still drinking, I was still clueless, and we were convinced that we had our stuff together after the near miss due to my "affair" at work a couple of years earlier. We felt that we had dodged a bullet, and we were now smart enough not to make *that* mistake again.

We were communicating better with each other, very appreciative of one another, and both agreed we really wanted our partnership to work. Other couples around us were "crashing and burning," and we were committed that we were *not* going to go there! So when asked to do the Marriage Encounter, at first we said, "Thanks, but no thanks. We're good."

However, another couple from our church whom we knew well and respected talked us into it. They had already done a weekend and "swore by it," as the expression goes.

Well—we went. But as far as we were concerned, we thought that we failed the program. After listening to each of the talks given during the encounter, we would go to our room, sit in overstuffed chairs with our feet up on the bed, and discuss what we had each written while answering the questions in our dialog packets. It felt like we were at a board meeting.

One of the three couples that ran the seminar, really left an impact on our hearts. We ended up becoming very close to them and their children for a few years until they moved to New Orleans. The odd thing was that even though they were involved in putting on the retreats and giving talks about how to improve relationships, they themselves were struggling. Actually, I guess I *can* understand since we, too, thought we had it so together.

At the time, we were totally unaware of why God had brought us to a marriage seminar, but as I move into the next part of the story, you will see how our lives were about to be reborn.

Andy Hits Bottom
August 17, 1985

In spring 1983, Andy mentioned to a coworker that he had given up drinking for Lent. That coworker chose to break his anonymity and gave Andy a meeting directory for Alcoholics Anonymous. Andy tossed it into his glove compartment and went on with life.

On a Wednesday in December, 1983, Andy attended his first AA meeting. It scared the crap out of him. He didn't believe he was "as sick as *those* folks."

Then in May of 1984, he attended his first White House retreat. The White House is a Jesuit retreat center that sits in a beautiful setting on a high bluff overlooking the Mississippi River. While there, Andy confided to a priest that he might have a drinking problem. Father connected him with a fellow he knew in the program who took Andy to another AA meeting; but Andy continued a journey of denial for a bit longer, going to AA meetings and then drinking on the way home.

Even though we attended another Marriage Encounter in the fall of 1984, he continued to vacillate about sobriety.

In May, 1985, Andy attended his second White House retreat, and the same priest who had tried to help him the first time once again provided the name and phone number of someone in the program. August 13 of the same year, Andy finally connected with that guy. Four days later, he surrendered.

On August 17, 1985, almost twenty months after his introduction to twelve-step recovery, Andy attended his first *sober* AA meeting, and his journey to recovery finally began. On August 17th of *this* year (2018), Andy celebrated thirty-three years of sobriety!

Let me tell you what it was like living with a "French waiter" drunk. We coined the term "French waiter," because I had no idea that Andy had a drinking problem. Therefore, his actions for the most part seemed normal. A French waiter may very well have a "buzz on"—not be "falling down" drunk—but sustain just enough of a "high" to carry on with his job.

I had had plenty of experience living with a dysfunctional family; but back then, I didn't know that it wasn't normal to have your father sneak into your room at night. I suppose I thought everyone had things they were ashamed about.

In Andy's case, he seemed normal. I wouldn't have known what to look for anyway. My idea of drunks was those vagrants I'd seen publicly staggering in unsavory parts of town.

Once when I was a kid and we still lived in north St. Louis, a drunk came down the street, and I didn't even have the sense to run.

The next thing I know, he grabbed me and was trying to drag me into a building. Fortunately, my mother opened the front window and started screaming and cussing at him to let me go. Then, the police came out of nowhere and arrested him.

Another time, when I happened to walk past a bedroom (again, still in north St. Louis, so I would have been less than nine years old), my dad's half-brother, Uncle Charlie, was sleeping on a bed. He didn't have a stitch on! No covers, nothing! I don't know how long I stood there mesmerized, before I realized I shouldn't be looking at this. I had no idea that he had come home drunk and passed out on the bed.

So, because Andy wasn't exhibiting *those* kinds of behavior, I never made the connection. He went to work every day and handled problems around the house just like he always had.

As a matter-of-fact, once, years later just before Andy finally sobered up, I was walking down the hall towards the kitchen, and Andy was at the kitchen sink with his back to me. Suddenly, he started chocking! I ran over and started to pat him on the back. Then he started turning blue—he couldn't catch his breath. He was coughing so hard he dropped to the floor. I asked him if he wanted me to call an ambulance, and he nodded his head yes. Then I was *really* scared because I knew he wasn't clowning around! Nothing like that had ever happened before.

When the emergency crew finally got there, they loaded him into the ambulance and *moseyed* (what seemed to be the longest route) all the way to the hospital. I was frantically following along behind in my car, beside myself, because in *my* mind, I figured he had already died, so they saw no reason to hurry.

Apparently, what happened was that while they were loading him on the stretcher into the ambulance, they must have jostled him enough so that he released a gas bubble; and when they got a whiff of it, they knew exactly what was wrong.

He had been guzzling a beer as he heard me coming down the hall, and the rest is history. But it did the trick as far as scaring me half to death.

When The Student Is Ready, The Teacher Will Come (Recovery Sneaks Up On Me)
1987

In 1987, I went to my first weekly twelve-step ACA (Adult Children of Alcoholics) meeting to deal with my incest issues. After the suggested six weeks, I diagnosed myself as "well" and quit.

In 1989, four years after Andy had already joined AA, his sponsor suggested that *he* try ACA. The sponsor surmised that Andy was having family-of-origin issues. After he had been attending for a while, I asked him if I could start coming to ACA meetings with him. I thought it was something "cute" we could do together.

Listening to the speaker that first day, I was so moved that I had to go to the ladies' room to compose myself. When I returned to the conference room, the meeting had ended and Andy was talking to the speaker. When he started to introduce me to her, I lost my composure again. The women stood there and held me while I sobbed for ten minutes, even though she had never met me before.

Before he got sober, I became very aware that Andy had a serious problem and apparently felt no need to address it. Near the end, it got to where I had lost all respect for him. I found it embarrassing to go to parties and watch him sitting on a straight-back chair across the room, swaying back and forth while I waited for him to drop off the chair and humiliate me yet again.

Once he literally got undressed at a party and crawled into the hosts' bed. I wanted him dead! I couldn't understand why he had no self-control. The booze took charge!

After some time in program, I eventually started to understand more about how cunning, baffling and powerful the disease of alcoholism is! If you've never been exposed to twelve-step principles, you may never understand what you can do to help (rather than hinder!) the situation. Many partners do even more damage to their relationship with an alcoholic because they have no concept about the disease of alcoholism.

I've learned that I can't change anyone but myself. My job is to work my program, and to be responsible for my actions. The coping skills I learned as a child no longer work. I discovered how to keep a conscious contact with God, who is not *out there* somewhere, but resides *INSIDE* of me.

I've turned my life and my will over to Him. I count on my sponsor (an experienced twelve-step program member) to give me honest feedback. Sometimes it hurts. And *some* hurts, real or imagined, might just be because **I'm the one** off base. I've learned that hurting people *hurt* people. It's not always about me. And I've learned about H.A.L.T. (hungry, angry, lonely, tired). I add an "S" at the end for sick, or P.M.S. or shitty.) I need to know how to recognize these H.A.L.T.S. pitfalls and take care of myself. We can't operate on all cylinders when we are suffering from one or more of these five physical/emotional conditions.

I've learned that *acceptance* is the answer to **all** my problems. Most times, *my* will (*ego*) causes me to edge God out. Instead, I've developed **being-ness** (being one with my Higher Power). I've learned that love is a **choice** *and* a **verb.** If I don't like the way I'm being treated, I need to look at the way I'm treating others.

Sometimes when I think "pissed is better," I just need to be willing, just **be willing**, to let it go.

I learned that just because my primary childhood caregivers were unhealed, I don't need to buy into the notion that I am nothing, or a mistake, or that "I'm bad." I learned forgiveness starts with me. And when I forgive, my world is a more beautiful place. I'm grateful for my life *and* its gifts.

I rely heavily on God and prayer. Some of my favorite prayers are simple. "Come Holy Spirit." "Thank you, God" (*Thk U-Gd* was also on my license plate). "Way to go God!" "Help me to accept!" These short phrases have become mantras that I've learned to say often as a knee-jerk reaction to help me keep my cool. They come in very handy when I'm excited, upset and/or needing to talk directly to God.

Sometimes, when I'm really out of joint, I imagine the Holy Spirit (whom I believe to be a woman) saying through clenched teeth, "Will you just give me time to finish the *to-do list* you have me working on now?" It makes me smile, because I know She's just kidding.

Mini-Community
1988

In 1988, we received a letter from our home parish, St. Joseph's, explaining that because the congregation was so big, many of the parishioners did not know each other. They were asking if we would be interested in having a wine and cheese party in our home, inviting twenty-five couples (fellow parishioners from our neighborhood) for an evening get-together.

We agreed. The first night we had more food than people. But we persisted. Eventually, we had a very close group of enthusiastic participants. We met on a regular basis at rotating homes.

At that time, three of us were stay-at-home moms. We became like the three musketeers. I would get phone calls from the church office telling me things like, "We have a single mom with five kids. If she doesn't get a stove and refrigerator by Monday, her children are going to be taken from her."

In that instance, it just so happened our next "wine and cheese" meeting was the same evening. I walked in and announced the dilemma this mother was facing. Three hands went up. "I have your stove." "I have your refrigerator." And, from one of the guys, "I have a truck, we can deliver!"

Another day I got a message that a young stewardess needed to talk to me. When I returned her call, she explained that she had recently been in an accident and was wearing a "halo" (a wire cage that was screwed into her head). She had received a perfect attendance award prior to her accident. It was a free roundtrip plane ticket. She wouldn't be able to use it and didn't want it to go to waste. "Could I help?"

Almost immediately afterwards, a young man phoned me. His best friend was being ordained to become a priest in another state and couldn't afford transportation. "Could I help?" So I hooked him up on a conference call with the stewardess. She was crying, he was crying, and I was crying!

You can't make this stuff up, folks! When we open ourselves to having God work through us, hold on to your hat because life will become *very* interesting!

Another time, I got a call from the parish office telling me that we had an older parishioner whose wife was in the hospital. He could no longer drive. Could we work something out to take him to the hospital? I put an APB out, and before you knew it, we had five or six gals who rotated taking him to the hospital to visit his wife.

God was always dropping things like that into our laps. How could we *not* believe in Him? I can remember, so often, calling the musketeers (one or the other) and asking, "Are you ready for our next assignment?"

Somehow, we met a guy in north St. Louis named Orville who ran a free thrift shop out of his home. He put canned goods on a table out in front of his house for anyone who needed them. He received his stock through donations and was simply passing it along to those who needed help. He did the same with chopped wood. Many in that area needed all the support they could get. So, our mini-community group went on a campaign of collecting coats and shoes for his mission.

One thing that was very unusual about Orville, was that he had several sons, four or five, all named Orville! Recently we discovered that he subsequently added a daughter to his family, and her name is Orville as well! Unfortunately, Orville Senior passed away about two years ago, but I'll bet he's watching from on high as his children carry on his mission.

Then we hit on the idea of coming up with women who would be willing to make a dish for the bereaved after a funeral. "Helping Hands" was born. It is now almost forty years old and still going strong! Run by a younger generation, though.

One Christmas, we decided to donate presents to a neighboring church for needy families. We would always pick the largest families, and truth be told, we went a little crazy. Buying on sale and using coupons, before we knew it our donations were overflowing over the allotted space into all direction.

One of the last things we did before the group fell apart was the most profound one for me. I like to think that God knew it was time for us to move on to something else. The group's demise happened due to hardships we couldn't anticipate, or repair.

Andy and I were co-chairs for the annual sausage supper at our parish that year. It just so happened that one of our sons, Scott, volunteered as a crewmember for a woman who owned a hot-air balloon. With Scott's help, we got her to donate several hours of tethering her balloon at the function. Tethering is when the balloon is still anchored to the ground so that it doesn't float away. The kids didn't care that it only went up and down. They lined up as far as the eye could see for their turn.

At that time, we had a pastor who was dearly loved by all. Father Jerry was carrying out his priestly duties dealing with lupus and, later, cancer. Unbeknownst to us, he had always wanted to go up in a hot-air balloon.

The morning of the event, as Father was genuflecting before leaving the altar at the finish of Mass, he broke his foot. Weak bones are a characteristic of his illnesses. Upon returning from the hospital, he was still very interested in going for a ride in that balloon, cast and all! The wind was picking up, causing the balloon owner some concern; and she wasn't certain the rides would be able to continue. But we told him to go get something to eat, and someone would come after him if, and when, it was time.

Our son, Scott, got to be the bearer of good news that the ride would happen. When he came back from delivering his message, he was laughing hysterically. He said, "Mom, you won't believe it, but Father Jerry is eating with a fork in each hand!" It took three men and a boy to get Father into that gondola (he was a big man to start with, plus a cast up to the knee didn't help matters). He was so happy, he could have eaten a banana sideways! When he came down after his "ride" and we finally got him settled down, the last words he said to me were, "Mary, I could die tomorrow, and I would go a happy man!" Three months later he was gone!

His successor was no Father Jerry. Without going into the particulars, the next pastor succeeded in alienating a large number of parishioners. I will leave it at that. What I *will* say is, he's the reason that I left the church for a time.

He Proposes
1989

In January, 1989, we reached our twenty-fifth wedding anniversary. Andy took me on a cruise. I would love to say that it was the most memorable time of my life. It actually *was*, but not for the reason you might think. I get sea sick! And I couldn't wait for the cruise to be over. My one nice memory that didn't include throwing up every twenty minutes *did* make the trip worth the discomfort!

We were sitting in one of those basket swings built-for-two that hang from the upper deck. We were just talking and enjoying each other's company when Andy starts to pull something from his pocket. Now you've got to picture this.

First of all, it's tight in those swings. I think that's on purpose. Of course, Andy and I are sitting down. He is wearing a pair of snug white jeans, and he is trying to pull something from his pocket. It wasn't budging. I had no idea what was in the pocket, but he sure was struggling. Trying not to embarrass him, I turned to look out at the sea. Keep in mind, there is nothing to see out there except the horizon bobbing up and down, which wasn't exactly curbing my seasickness.

What seemed like hours later, he softly says, "Charlie?" (his nickname for me). I turn to see him holding an open jeweler's box in his hand, complete with ring! And he says, "Will you marry me?" Completely shocked and surprised, I sat there with my mouth hanging open for what must have been an uncomfortable amount of time, because he asked again, "Charlie? Do I need to repeat the question?"

To say that I was stunned would be an understatement. I was also confused, we have already been married for twenty-five years. What's the deal? Then he explains to me, "We married in such a hurry the first time, with Mark being on the way, I knew you believed that I just married you because it was the right thing to do. This is to prove I married you because I wanted to, not because I felt I HAD to. And this was the only way I could think of to get you to understand that I was in this for the long haul right from the beginning!"

And he was absolutely right! Sure, we ran into rough spots every now and then, but there isn't a marriage in the world without rough spots. He just wanted me to know that my being pregnant when we got married was NOT one of them.

And, I have to admit that in the beginning, I resented it every time he disciplined Mark. I thought he was doing it because he thought of Mark as a millstone around his neck—if it weren't for Mark, he wouldn't have had to marry me. Imagine what that must have done to

Mark! It could explain a lot of things about Marks's relationship with the family. I'm sure the fact that I leaned so heavily on him to help me parent his siblings didn't help matters any.

    Have you ever had times in your life when you wished you would have done things differently? Looking back on how Mark must have felt growing up is something I would give ANYTHING to change.

How We Got Into Prison
1989

Also in 1989, Andy finally met one of his clients face to face for the first time. They had been doing business together for three years by phone. Plans to play golf in northeast Missouri (the client's neck of the woods) would be a great opportunity.

After the golf game, they were lounging on the ground under a tree when they got into a conversation regarding what they did in their spare time. Turns out the client was involved with a group from his church that took retreats into prisons.

That night, while we lay in bed talking about our day, Andy tells me this story. Then he says to me, "Tony's going to call me to participate when they have another retreat."

The next thing I know, I'm sitting up on my knees in bed practically screaming at him, "You lucky stiff, you get to go into the big house! I want to go, too!" Then I stopped, looked around and said, "Who said that?" He started laughing, and replied, "You did!" This coming from a gal who when scheduled to go on a high school field trip "behind the walls" in Jefferson City was nervous as a long-tailed cat in a room full of rockers. The day we went, I forgot to put on a slip and wore my coat all day, even when inside, because I was afraid the inmates could see through my skirt, and I might cause a riot! Naturally, (just my luck!) it turned unseasonably warm that day.

We Just Kept Going Back To Prison
1990–1994

True to his word, the client contacted Andy when the next retreat started their formation to see if Andy was serious about getting involved. He was thrilled to find out that I had also expressed an interest. The first time we went in, we were observers in the Renz Prison in Jefferson City, Missouri. It was like a dry run to see if we could handle it. We had no idea what to expect. But we were both hooked from the get-go!

I remember walking up to a table to which I had been assigned, and directly across from me was a guy sitting in a tee shirt with a pack of cigarettes rolled up in the sleeve. His arms were tattooed from the shoulder to the fingertips. There were other guys sitting all the way around the table, with only one empty seat for me; but the tattooed man was all I saw at that moment. My first thought was, "What have I gotten myself into?"

His name was John, and by the end of that weekend I remember saying to him, "If there was anyone here that I would pick out as the epitome of John the Baptist, it would be you!" Snap judgments can sure come back to bite us.

The second time we went in, it was to Mt. Sterling in Illinois, and I remember reading signs everywhere that said, "If you hear shots fired, sit down immediately." A lot of us were making jokes like, "If I hear shots, they're going to have to dig up the sidewalk to find me!" We never heard shots, and they never had to look for us.

We usually gave our talks as a couple. Or maybe it was just taken for granted. In the beginning, we were nervous, but we remember them telling us not to worry. It really didn't matter much what we said, "That we could recite the alphabet to them and they would hear what they each needed to hear."

The inmates listened to us with great interest—apparently they DID hear what they needed to hear—and a new pattern started. After each talk, they treated us as if we were celebrities! They lined up to ask questions and couldn't wait to share similarities that we might have. Or tell us exactly what we said that got their attention. They couldn't wait to hear us again and wanted to know when we were coming back. Fortunately, neither of us let it go to our heads as we knew that it wasn't us "ringing their chimes," it was the Holy Spirit using us as a channel, and we couldn't feel more honored.

Andy and I both believe strongly in marriage and that part of our journey is to show others how awesome marriage can be! Yes, it's work, but oh-so-worth-it! When you do it right, the analogy I like to use is making a snowman together. At first, you must work at it, learn each other's little idiosyncrasies and how to deal with them, but when you do, your snowball is big enough that you can just roll it down the hill, picking up more snow as it picks up steam!

This doesn't mean that we never had problems, as you already read about. But we learned from our mistakes and adjusted as best we could with the understanding that we are ***committed*** to the relationship; and in the end, we will still be standing! Together!

In our twenty-sixth anniversary year (which was 1990), we spoke at Missouri Eastern Correction Center (MECC for short), the prison closest to our home. Up until now, we had been limiting ourselves to two or three retreats a year. We were afraid that we would suffer burn-out if we went in more often. Besides, there was no shortage of volunteers, as some of them went in every chance they got!

The most memorable aspect about our first talk at MECC was while we were speaking at the podium, a picture of Christ was hanging behind us on the wall. It has always been my favorite because it's of Christ behind bars. So many times, I see Christ in those men. Suddenly, right in the middle of our presentation, the picture dropped off the wall! Without thinking, the words, "Is this the best you can do?" came out of my mouth. The guys loved it! They knew that I was talking to the devil!

How I Met Sue McClure
1991

When God is ready, He can move with great speed! Three things came very close together for me—going to the ACA meetings on my own (no one pushing me); getting involved in the prison ministry with Residents Encounter Christ (REC) retreat weekends; and this next incident I'm about to relay—all prepared me for God to make His move in my life. And I guess *I* was finally ready.

I had been interviewing therapists for some time. I knew that I wanted a woman, preferably someone who understood the twelve-step programs, and someone who had a faith life. What I was running into were some "strange folks." I would start out the conversation the same way each time, "I'm looking for someone who can help me heal from a bad childhood. I do *not* want to give it a lick and a promise, I'm serious and ready and able to do whatever you tell me I need to do." And by the way, I do not want to grow old with you, nor buy you a new house! But I will do the work!"

The only answer I remember was this one guy telling me, "I can have you well in six weeks!"

My comment to him on my way out the door was, "Yeah, right!"

Then one day, one of the guys from my twelve-step meeting came up to me and said, "I understand that you're looking for a therapist."

"Yes, I am, do you have someone in mind?"

"I sure do, she used to be my therapist, until she and my wife started working in the same office. That caused a conflict of interest so I had to stop seeing her."

Our first interview was by phone. We talked for some time, and she met the criteria, except that she was younger, which I hadn't anticipated. However, she was very well-grounded and fit the bill to a tee. God works like that. He likes to throw you a curve ball every once in a while.

After talking for some time that evening, she suddenly asked, "What are you doing now?"

"Talking to you," I quipped.

She laughed, and then said, "No, what I mean is, are you busy?"

"No," I answered, "Why do you ask?"

"Why don't you come over to my office? I don't have anyone scheduled this evening, we can meet face to face and see how the chemistry works," then she topped it all off, by adding, "*No charge.*"

I knew right then that she wasn't in it for the money!

I saw Sue on a regular basis, and what she did was ask me questions that pulled the scabs I had built over the years off their wounds. I would answer her questions to the best of my ability, my memory was much better then. She would help put things into a perspective that not only made sense but assisted me in understanding that I wasn't usually the one at fault in the situation. Or, she would give me another way of looking at what had happened. I would go home raw, but also elated! I would call Andy, and we would meet wherever it was convenient for the two of us so we could talk without the kids (who were now teenagers) around.

Processing the work with a trusted confidant (Andy) in between sessions with the therapist was almost as important as the work done with the counselor. We would meet in the car, if there was no other place close and safe, or in the park if the weather was nice. We met as soon as possible so that I could remember all of the many details discussed. This sharing was also helping Andy and me to come even closer as a couple. He was going through his own therapy with someone else. The insights I was sharing about myself were allowing him to learn everything there was to know about me.

She helped me to understand that I didn't have to be ashamed of my past. And at the same time, Andy would share things about himself with me, so I was learning more about him, too! Many of the confidences Andy divulged helped me feel even better about myself. The more we know our partners, the closer we become, and the freer we feel. We must reveal to heal!

Something I want you to understand—I told Andy about my dad as soon as I realized that we were becoming serious about each other. I wanted Andy to know that he was getting (what *I* believed to be) "damaged goods." The things I shared with him after being with Sue included her opinion on a situation and how she thought I should best handle it. I had never kept secrets from Andy. Almost everything I talked to Sue about was old news for him. But the more we tell it, the less it hurts!

Once for one of my sessions, I showed up with Andy in tow, and as we walked past her through the door, she nods her head in his direction and asks, "What's *he* doing here?"

Andy's answer was, "We're at a Mexican standoff, and we need a mediator."

Again, it was worked out in one session! Now, you tell me God didn't send her!

I have no idea how long Sue worked with me, but I can tell you this, it wasn't years. She has done two things that probably are unheard of for a therapist. First, she offered to work with our kids and their partners as well as with me. Second, she fired me! One day she said that she thought we had gone about as far as I needed to go at that point in time, but that if I ever felt differently, to just give her a call and we would work something out.

Occasionally, I may still call her with some issue that has me upset, and she will talk me "off the ledge" so to speak.

The most recent exchange we had was shortly after I was diagnosed with Alzheimer's. Andy's background was sales, and he excelled at it. A good salesman asks a lot of questions. One night he was questioning me about something, and I was getting more and more frustrated. I didn't know what was going on or why I was getting so upset, but I was feeling badgered.

So, I called Sue. After listening, without hesitation (as if she was waiting for my call), she said, "*Okay, get a piece of paper and something to write with.*"

Then she had me write down four things: 1) Ask only questions that can be answered *yes* or *no*; 2) Don't push for details; 3) Stop, listen *only*; and 4) Don't ask more questions.

Then she said, "This is for Andy to help him cope with your condition." And the beautiful thing he did was to put the four points into his phone so that he would have it at his fingertips.

What we learned is that too many questions confuse Alzheimer's patients and trigger our brains to shut down. We need time to let our minds take inventory and find the appropriate answer to the question. Multiple questions cause our head to short-circuit.

"THE" Break-Through Talk
1992

Each time we did a REC weekend at the prison, we grew emotionally and spiritually, both as individuals and as a couple.

To prepare for these weekends, the team of twenty-five (twelve couples and a priest) would meet and map out who would be presenting what talks. We would practice giving our talks to the team before we actually went in to do the retreat weekend.

At a team meeting when one of the other women gave her talk for us, she told my story. So many similarities were there, I broke down emotionally when I heard it. I knew I would soon be asked to give a talk, and apparently, some aspects of my life still needed healing.

When my turn to speak came a few months later, I wrote the 3500-word talk for the retreat in about three hours. Two days later, I gave it to the team, *verbatim*. It was a gorgeous sunny day. Except, just as I was telling the team parts of my life I had (up until that point) *never* shared with anyone except Andy, lightning struck the building! Talk about irony! I finished my talk to the tune of sirens blaring because apparently the lightning had caused a fire.

But afterwards, I felt great! Until Monday morning, when I received the phone call from the retreat director telling me that my talk was found "morally offensive."

"That was my life story, not some movie I was writing," I managed to gasp through my shock. "I wasn't making this stuff up! You have no right to judge my life! I finally worked up the courage to open myself, let people see into me, and share my secrets so that I can heal, and I'm found not good enough!?!"

I was livid! Crushed! And hurt, all at the same time! I felt so exposed!

Bottom line—I was given two choices. Either re-write the talk, or I was off the team. Long story short, I re-wrote the talk. However, I was never able to commit it to memory. What happened next was most amazing.

While giving the revised talk, I felt as though someone was standing at my left ear and saying to me, "Tell them about the time you met so and so." So, I did. Then, "Tell them about *this* . . . tell them about *that*."

Each time, I would relay the corresponding story. Finally, I looked down at my notes and realized that I had covered all the pertinent points. **But none of those stories were on the papers in front of me.** The Holy Spirit had led me through my talk.

The real beauty of it all was that the inmates ended up hearing *exactly* what they needed to hear. They were saying things like, "It was as though you were talking just to *ME*," or, "You helped me make a decision I have been wrestling with for a long time—thank you." Through no fault of my own, I had allowed myself to be a vessel for Spirit.

It wasn't until I got involved with Catholic ACTS Retreats in 2004, **eleven years later**, that I learned why God let that happen. But let's not jump the gun here.

A quick sidebar on that story—five team members, including me, ended up in therapy after the talk I did for the team prior to the REC retreat. Fortunately, I had already started seeing Sue McClure! Oh, I definitely needed to work through a grudge I held against those people on that team who made me rewrite my talk, even though it DID work out so well in the end.

Touched By An Angel?
1993

We often read stories in the Bible about how God used angels to speak to human beings. But was that just in biblical times . . . or does He continue to send us messages through angels today? I wonder, because I have trouble explaining one of my most moving life experiences in any other way.

By early July, 1993, our children were grown and had all flown the coop. Although I had worked several full or part-time jobs over the years, I was now feeling somewhat at loose ends. No doubt I perceived my life to be very blessed, in spite of the fact that things started out less than perfect. At this state, for the most part, it had come together quite nicely for my family and me. I had a notion that I needed to show my appreciation to God in some tangible way by giving back.

So, I scheduled a meeting with someone I thought was a nun to discuss the possibility of volunteer work—having no idea at the time what God had in store for me.

All I can remember about *this* experience is an approximate location of the meeting place. We were at Catholic College in St. Louis, and I can't even remember in what capacity I was applying to volunteer. This nun and I settled into a couple of comfortable, overstuffed chairs in the lobby of one of the main buildings. We must have been in an out-of-the-way place because I don't remember a lot of activity or any distracting noise.

I can't even tell you what she looked like. I have an impression of a typical nun dressed in a white, non-descript blouse and dark blue skirt with the usual short matching blue veil. Other than that, I could not pick her out of a line-up.

I do remember she was very soft-spoken, though she didn't say much, and her eyes were exceptionally kind. She started off the conversation by asking me to tell her about myself. I started out typically enough—describing how I'd been happily married to the same man for forty years—that Andy and I had raised four impressive, healthy children together.

But then, for some strange reason, I began revealing everything; and I do mean *everything*. The good—that our youngest (and only) daughter and one of our sons were recently married in the same calendar year—that all our now-grown children and their families were doing well. I told her about various jobs I had held and accomplishments I achieved. I told her about some of the skills I developed, and about other projects for which I had volunteered.

Without any prompting, I also found myself talking about the bad, too. I told her about some of the tough times we had experienced, and how we were overcoming them. I confessed my promiscuity as a young adult.

Before long I moved on to the ugly, particularly my husband's battle with alcoholism before he began to embrace recovery. Then I started talking about some of the really tough times, before my husband came into my life. I told her about having been engaged and losing my fiancé in an auto accident—easily the most emotionally painful blow ever.

Eventually, I even found myself telling the nun about the worst of times, the things that had happened to me while growing up. I described the nun in fourth grade who was physically and emotionally abusive and seemed to have a personal vendetta against me. I couldn't go to my parents, I said, because they thought I had done something to provoke her. Besides, they weren't the loving, nurturing kind of parents a kid could take her problems to—they had gone on to their Maker without having done their own emotional work.

Finally, I told her about a little girl's darkest fears—how I was afraid to go to bed at night because my father would sneak into my room—being terrified to take a bath because the bathroom door didn't have a lock. I also told her about my maternal-grandfather, who was just as sick as my father.

It became an extraordinary time, sitting across from the nun in that overstuffed chair. I felt as if my mouth had a mind of its own. Imagine having fallen and being unable to get up—except that my mouth hadn't fallen, it just wouldn't stop talking.

The entire time, she just sat there, never saying a word, gazing at me with those beautiful, soft, brown eyes, creating a safe atmosphere for me to go on and on. She *listened* my story out of me--just nodding her head as if she knew what I was going to say before I said it. My brain kept thinking, *"Shut Up! Shut up! Don't you realize that you are telling her things that only Andy, knows? This is a Catholic nun! What must she think of you?"* but my voice continued.

At some point she must have reached over and taken my hand, as if to say, "I'm here for you, it's okay, I am so sorry that those things happened to you."

And then suddenly, I burst into tears. When I was able to compose myself enough to talk, I croaked out, "Those *are* my gifts, aren't they?"

To which she softly replied, "Yes, they are. Our past *is* our gift." She went on to explain, "Even the ugliest times in our lives need not defeat us. It all depends at how we look at them. God never gives us more then we can handle. We have hard times so that when we work through them, we heal. When we heal, we become stronger in the broken places. When we become stronger, we're able to be there for others. We will someday be able to be there to listen to someone else going through their own pain as they attempt to heal."

In that totally unexpected conversation, I had a complete paradigm shift. I went from believing that I was worthless, to realizing that *I had a purpose*! God made me for a specific reason. My past was no longer to be a millstone around my neck! It was what I *needed* to experience to help someone else make the same connection when they heard my story! What was I supposed to do with that message? Eventually, I would come to learn.

The most important revelation during my talk with the nun (who I honestly believe was an angel sent to help me) was—I'm not a SURVIVOR of incest; I'm a **THRIVER** *of incest. I take what I've learned from that time in my life, and I make it work for me. I help others see it differently so that they, too, may experience a paradigm shift and see that God has a purpose for THEM!*

I'm Home - We Became V.I.C.'s[*]
1994

Had my "angel" messenger even been real? I didn't find the answer until a year (to the month!) later.

By July of 1994, we had quite a following of men on the inside. The guys would write to us through a P.O. Box. The numbers grew so large I had to go from answering each man individually to doing a monthly newsletter. We were now in touch with about a hundred and eighty-five guys from three different prisons in two states. It got so I didn't have time for anything else. Once again, God handled the problem for me.

In July 1994, I had gotten word from one of my many correspondents at MECC (the prison closest to our home) that the Institute Activities Coordinator (IAC) was looking for someone to volunteer as his assistant at the facility.

Exactly one year later, give or take a day, after my encounter with "the nun," I'm standing in the office of the IAC, who is explaining to me the job duties required of his assistant. The institute activities office oversees all the programming offered to the inmates. In most

---
[*] Volunteer In Corrections

cases if a guy takes a program, it's elective. However, some classes are mandatory.

Each time he outlined another aspect of the job, I would think, *"Did that before and loved it! I was really good at that! I have awards for doing that!"*

The last thing he said during the interview was, "It will be hard for some of these guys to trust you. They *know* THEY are not trustworthy, so they don't trust anyone else, especially women. If you want them to be open with you, you have to open up to them first."

In that moment, I realized I had been in training for this job since I was five years old.

Reasons became clear for why I went through all that heartache, pain and misery when I was younger. Why I since underwent all that therapy. Why I've been involved in bringing the retreats into the prisons. Why I'd met a mysterious nun who explained to me the meaning in all the "ugliest" moments of my life.

Yes, a heavenly messenger had spoken! *THIS* is why God made me! I would begin to work with prisoners.

I remember the IAC telling me that these guys are nothing more than big, hurting kids. Mostly, their lives left a lot to be desired and many of them are still reeling from the fallout. But the aspect that impacted me most was that they don't *trust*. I knew ALL about lack of trust! And *I* was going to have to trust enough to tell *them* about *me* in order to earn THEIR trust.

Because I understood how they felt, it seemed like music to my ears! I realized that God had just been waiting for the right time to put me here. As crazy as it sounds, I *knew* I was home from the very first day!

Look Out World, Here I Come... To Prison
1994–2003

At that time, the IAC had two inmates working with him. The office had only been set up three years earlier with a grocery bag of papers and one desk. Ever since then, they'd been scrounging for needed items to get the task done. But they were doing a bang-up job with what little they had.

The only downfall to my becoming what I prefer to call a "professional volunteer" was that because I was working so closely with state employees, Andy and I could no longer write to the inmates. It is considered "a conflict of interest." So, I had to sever ties with nearly two hundred pen pals. Besides, now I was so busy that I just didn't have *time* to write anymore.

However, I STILL regret not having been able to address that one last letter to the men with whom we had built written relationships. We made the commitment to follow all the rules and regulations as those of the full-time prison employees. We went through the same training as every paid employee did. We could not have any contact with the former inmates on the outside, or those still in other facilities, even though we'd been doing it regularly for a long time. We abided by the rules, but it has always bothered me that we were not awarded the opportunity for closure with those men, and they have no idea what happened to us. Just all of a sudden, our letters to them stopped coming.

For all they know, we died. Or worse yet, that we just gave up on them—like so many others in their lives who simply walked away. Trust is already a problem for them because they know they are not trustworthy, especially with women. Then, out of nowhere, we are gone and no one knows why. That regret kept me awake many a night!

The two inmate clerks who worked for the IAC (Dave) had the greatest respect for him. Even though I wasn't scared that the prisoners would hurt me, I knew those two clerks had our backs if need be. They welcomed me in as their big sister, even though these two guys were close to my age. Dave was fifteen years my junior, and he called me "Sissie." We quickly fell into a rhythm. As a team, "we kicked butt" (that's what the guys would say). I'm sure they cleaned it up a bit for my benefit.

It didn't take me long to learn that most of the men behind those bars are very lovable and would do anything for you if you treat them with dignity and respect. Don't get me wrong, they are still cons; and if they see an opportunity for a scam, they're going to take it! Before long, I was working twenty-five to thirty-five hours a week as Dave's VIC/IAC, as he liked to refer to me for short (Volunteer In Corrections/Institute Activity Coordinator).

We worked extremely well together. Co-workers who were made for each other (kind of like Andy and me!). We started all kinds of new programs and hired many volunteers to conduct said classes. Our prison had more programs and classes to help the men help themselves than any other facility. We became known as the *Going Home* prison! Often, Andy and I would be the ones to run certain classes and programs. That's how I learned that I love to teach.

After twelve years on the job, Dave's brother transferred back to MECC as the new warden, so Dave had to take a lateral move to Probation and Parole because he would have been in his brother's direct chain of command. In a government position, it's against regulations for relatives to report to one another.

Now, I had been doing Dave's job for nine years as a volunteer in the capacity of his assistant. I didn't care about the money. I was doing God's work and loving it!

Since I was the most logical person to take Dave's place (and came highly recommended), the new warden held the position open for three months while I was sent for training to officially learn the ropes. That's how our government works, folks!

On July 1, 2003, exactly nine years to the day after Andy and I became official volunteers, I assumed the paid IAC position, a job for which I never even applied! Being the "big cheese" seemed incredible to me.

I loved what I was doing, but I found I really missed my "big brother," Dave. He had always reminded me of a large St. Bernard puppy.

He was so sweet to me. One day he thought an inmate was trying to harm me. He got so mad that he had his hands (they looked like ham hocks!) on each side of the door frame and pushed so hard he was actually able to bow the metal frame out of shape.

Another time, an inmate was very upset and crying in Dave's office. When I peeked in, Dave was crying right along with the man.

And then there was the time he asked me, "Sissie, why does everyone keep calling me Davey?" I just smiled and said, "Gee, I don't know Davey." Our loss was Probation and Parole's gain.

One of my favorite parts of the new job was doing one-on-one sessions with the men. My major was psychology in college, and I always wanted to put a "Lucy" sign out for the guys that were hurting and needed to talk. So, the clerks made a little flag from PCP pipe and a piece of bright yellow felt to put on top of my computer monitor to let everyone know when I was in session. "Stay away," the flag said,

"Someday it will be your turn." All of this unscheduled counseling activity transpired during business hours, but the amazing thing was the rest of the office work always got done.

We started a twelve-step self-help meeting. In the beginning, there was me and two inmates. Eventually, it had to be split into two meetings on different days. If you went to the Friday morning meeting, you couldn't go to the one on Tuesday afternoons. There was an occupancy limit in the meeting room, and we wanted to reach as many people as possible. Both meetings were filled to capacity every single week.

We had ten other twelve-step meetings a week. These were in addition to the programs or classes like Financial Peace, Breaking Barriers, Youth Awareness Group, and a multitude of others. Eventually, they even brought in a "Puppies on Parole" program, which involved the inmates training stray dogs to be adoptable. A win/win all the way around. I think the men and the dogs really felt a connection with each other.

We came up with some amazing concepts and somehow managed to get them all done. Those men are genius material, and I tell them that all the time. I always knew they were God's ideas because He really wanted these men to figure out for themselves that they were *never* stupid. Through *them*, God was going to make everything happen. He just let me help.

God was pulling *all* the strings here. When I first started at that prison, it was predominately inhabited by sex offenders. Should have been a frightening proposition for someone with my background! However, over the years, I have been able to see these men through compassionate eyes--as wounded children themselves in men's bodies. Whatever they have done to others to deserve incarceration was either done to them, or they've seen it done by someone close to them. I learned to have great empathy for them. Polar opposite of the woman I used to be who wanted every sex offender castrated.

The fact is—those men helped further my healing through listening to their stories—a side benefit I never expected. I was able to recognize what dysfunction had done to them. When I heard their history, I understood *why* they perpetrated their crimes. And as a bonus blessing, I also began to understand my father and grandfather's behavior from *their* perspective, and I was able to forgive. *Really* forgive!

How To Keep Love Alive

Andy had been sober in twelve-step recovery for about nine years at this point. I was relieved, but part of me was still afraid that this wouldn't last. It takes a long time to trust when the rug has been pulled out from under you.

One of the things I believe really helped me to get back "in step" (pun intended!) with Andy was watching Oprah Winfrey's daily TV show. I had never watched daytime television in my life, but somehow (no coincidences!) I got hooked on this one.

Right about this time, Oprah was on an *improve yourself* kick. She was encouraging all her viewers to become the best version of ourselves we could be. A lot of guests appeared on the show, each with their own ideas that we could incorporate into our self-improvement journey. To me, this was a God-send!

One of the suggestions that really resonated with me was the idea of keeping a gratitude journal. Each night before going to bed, we were to write down in a notebook five things that we noticed that day for which we were thankful. So, I thought, *What the heck, what could it hurt?*

That exercise started me on a project that lasted several years. I had no idea how skewed my thinking had become while living with active alcoholism! Apparently, I was very disgruntled with Andy's drinking and his self-absorption. Even though he now had almost nine years of sobriety, I was still waiting for the other shoe to drop.

Because these are the only ones I can remember, I'll share these two samples of some of my gratitude journal entries:
- Thank you, God, for not letting me cut Andy's heart out today and hand it to him.
- Thank you, God, for not letting me bite Andy's jugular and watch him bleed to death.

I was not proud of my thinking, then or now. However, I was very unhappy and needed some way to rid myself of these negative thoughts.

I never allowed anyone to see what I was writing because even in my irrational thinking at the time, on some logical level I knew others could never understand how angry, frustrated, lonely and full of hate I had become. At the same time, *I* couldn't fathom how you could love someone so much and have it turn so quickly to what I was feeling at that time. Some nights, I would try with all my might (to no avail) to come up with something *positive*.

What I didn't realize until much later was that I *needed* to write down all those terrible things in order to purge the anger, frustration and venom out of me!

I was determined to do it *every* night. Sometimes I would sit there for long periods, simply trying to tap into the favorable. Ever so gradually, it began to change; and I softened. Or maybe he was trying harder—I don't know—undoubtedly it was a combination of both. But eventually, I started to see a side of him I had never noticed before. Somewhere during this time is when I started consistently asking the Holy Spirit for help, and She *always* came through for me!

Because I knew I had to come up with five *affirmative* things every night for my journal, I started paying more attention to what was Andy *actually* doing, rather than allowing my old perception habits to prevail. Before I knew it, I started noticing little things he did to show me he was thinking of me and/or the kids rather than *himself* all the time. I was blown away!

Slowly I was learning that you *get* what you *focus on*. If you pay attention to the positive, you will get the positive. Whereas when you focus on the negative, guess what you'll get? You guessed it!

I wish I had a dollar for every time I've caught myself saying, "I need to find those journals before I die. I don't want the kids to run across them after I'm gone—what will they think of me?!" I didn't ever want them to find out that I had hated their father so much. Then one day, the thought hit me—maybe that's *not* such a bad thing, because the kids absolutely know us the way we are now, and the only thing we argue about is which of us loves the other one more!

Perhaps if one of them ever runs into a rough spot in their own relationship, they will remember reading some of my old journals. It just might give them the incentive to fight to make it right. I've known many troubled couples who have hung in there and reconciled, remaining together. Relationships are ALWAYS stronger in the broken places if you are able to work through them! I believe it's God's way of rewarding us for hanging in there and giving our best, which is all He asks from His children.

It didn't happen overnight. But it did happen. It's so much clearer now—all that time, I was still in God's hands, and he knew how much I was hurting, but he also knew how much Andy was hurting.

That's why people try to anesthetize themselves. Andy's drug of choice was booze. Mine was self-pity!

Something I learned in program and from my prison ministry work is, "Hurting people, hurt people." Andy came into the relationship with his own "bag of worms" (the expression I like to use for all the little idiosyncrasies we create to help us deal with life). I had mine own, as well.

Each of our families of origin plays a huge part in who we become and what happens to us. The meaning we attribute to our background generally dictates the roadmap of who we will become and how we look at life.

It doesn't *always* play itself out in the same way in our various relationships. But the repercussions from our life experiences and the significances we put on those occurrences are huge.

Andy was dealing with his own issues, and I was trying to cope with mine. Unfortunately, we weren't working as a team, to say the least.

After working with the journals for a while, (after several years of faithfulness to this practice, I filled up quite a few!), we slowly started coming together. We began complimenting each other on the nice things we did for each other, the kids or anyone in our circle of friends. Eventually, we fell back in *like* with each other. I say "like" because I think we were always in love. The description we once heard of "love" is that it is a *decision*. We were committed to each other from the beginning, making a pact which we honored to NEVER use the "D" word, divorce. It only erodes the relationship and leaves our partner wondering if he/she is sitting on a time bomb. It breeds a sense of "why bother?" if one foot is already out the door! The fact is, I *did* sign up for "until death do us part" and I *knew* I didn't have it in me to kill him!

When I got off track with that guy from work, it was because we were not focusing on each other anymore. We had fallen into a trap that many couples do by taking each other for granted. Never thinking to go out of our way to romance or do special things for each other.

I can tell you this—today there is *no one*, not any movie star or charismatic personality, who could catch me in that trap again!

Fortunately for us, God had stepped in, bringing that third person onto the equation to really wake us up. It scared us enough to re-think our priorities. If we're not getting our needs met, we need to first check and see if we are meeting our partner's needs. And if we're not sure, ask him or her! Communication is key.

Something we used to do is called "tank check." This is when one of us would ask the other, on a scale of one to ten (one being lousy and ten awesome), where would you rate our relationship? If the answer is anything less than a 7, the next question is what can I do to fill the tank? The tank is our "love tank"—how much we *feel* loved. Often *I* think I'm doing things right, but it's not my opinion that counts, it's Andy's. So often we criticize or correct our partners without even thinking about it, leaving them feeling hurt or resentful. Our daily input to each other should *build up* rather than *tear down*.

We got this idea from Gary Chapman, who wrote *The Five Love Languages*. And we will both highly recommend it to any and all of our friends struggling in their relationships. It even works to improve relationships between people who don't think they are struggling.

When we start complaining about our partners and how they are not meeting our needs, we are setting ourselves up for a fall. ***An expectation is a resentment waiting to happen.*** Read that again, slowly. Then think about it for a minute before going on.

Our partners can't possibly know what we have on our minds, unless we tell them. Even then, they may not remember because it's not as important to them as it is to us. I personally believe for men, it's even tougher than it is for women. For one, men don't think like women do—some things simply don't occur to them. Not only that, but they don't seem to have as many needs as women do.

Give a guy a good hot meal at least once a day, **five** compliments for every **one** criticism, and sex a couple of times a week; and he's a happy camper!

On the other hand, here's how women think:
- He needs to know what I am thinking without my telling him.

- He should do things for me **_exactly_** the way I would do it.
- I shouldn't have to ask him to do what I need him to do.
- He should verbally tell me how much he appreciates what I do for him. (Even though I will probably forget to thank *him* because I expect him to just do "it" whatever "it" is.)

Pay attention here--the reason the above bullet points are not likely to happen is because *our brains are not even built to work the same way*. A male brain is compartmentalized, like a bee hive. They have one thought at a time. They can actually block everything other than the one thought they want to work on. Our brains have a multi-highway system that crisscrosses from one lobe to the other and back again multiple times in a very small space and time frame.

Most couples don't have a clue as to how the brains work, much less any idea of the vast differences between the two genders.

I believe that if every couple HAD to complete a six-week course on the differences between male and female brains, it might just cut down the divorce rate.

For a period of about two years, I had to use a mantra, "*He lives here too, he helps pay the bills.*" I would repeat this to myself on a regular basis, just to keep from going "postal" on him when he didn't do something the way I thought he should.

Sometimes I forget, and I have to put myself through re-training for a while until I can remember to back off and be content with the way he does things. When I am able to do this, I allow myself to drop all my expectations; and I am almost *always* pleasantly surprised with our results!

A prime example—ever since we have been plagued with this Alzheimer's thing, Andy has pretty much taken over the cooking. And he is doing an awesome job!

I have not had one bad meal! I do, however, keep telling Andy that I am pretty ticked with him for holding out his culinary talents for almost fifty-five years.

Life gets better as we go!

Once we realized it was easier and more fun to work *together* as opposed to always honing in on each other's faults, we wanted to share this stuff. We started reading books and magazines, and listening to podcasts, on healthy relationships. One of the books that left a real impact was John Gray's *Men are from Mars, and Women are from Venus*.

We kept a copy of the book on the coffee table and referred to it as the "other Bible." Eventually we started giving it as a three-part gift for weddings to which we were invited.

The second of the three parts is a goblet with a piece of paper rolled up in it that essentially says, "By filling this goblet with water I am offering an apology to you. This is a way of enacting truces without saying a word. If the partner accepts and drinks the water, it is their unspoken way of accepting the apology and at the same time asking forgiveness for any part he/she played in the process." It's a beautifully symbolic rite, and one which works like a charm if used faithfully.

The third part to our wedding gift is a cross. Obviously representing Christ.

Andy made a beautiful wedding card explaining each piece and that the gift signified a rope made with three strands. It is woven together and almost impossible to break. Each strand stands for someone—God, the bride and the groom. Those who remember to keep God at the center of their relationship will make it!

Marriage is not for sissies. Unfortunately, so many jump into matrimony without a clue as to how to make it work. It is, undisputedly, THE toughest relationship; but, when done right, THE most rewarding one.

Eventually, we went to California and studied under John Gray to become facilitators for his workshops. Then we started presenting his theme in our home for other couples. If you really want to learn to do something well, try teaching it!

Later on, we also started teaching couples "Cash Flow," a game based on managing money, that then grew into "Financial Peace University," which is still done at our church twice a year and also at the prison. The inmates LOVE it!

Ninety-three percent of marriages that fail break up because both partners are NOT on the same wavelength regarding money. One is usually a saver while the other is a spender. Not a good combination for a marriage, but with communication and compromise, couples CAN make it work.

Over the years, we have been involved in several small groups of couples wanting to keep their marriages strong. We would meet together regularly to work on problems or come up with ideas to keep our relationships fresh. What a rewarding gift to witness struggling couples find the spark again.

Another thing we do faithfully is attend **at least** one weekend marriage retreat and/or seminar annually.

It's like maintaining your car—if you want to keep it running, you have to give it the proper care and attention!

We have never considered *any* idea for improving our marriage a waste of time or money, including therapy!

The Life Adventure Continues
A Promise Is A Promise
Spring 2001

I want to relay an impressive experience we had on our way home from an Anthony Robbins "Date With Destiny" seminar in Miami.

It happened because of another motivational speaker we had been following since 1978 named Wayne Dyer. He wrote a book about a woman, Kaye, and her daughter, Edwarda. The book was called *A Promise Is A Promise*.

Edwarda fell prey to a diabetic coma at the age of sixteen and was in a vegetative state for over forty-two years. Her mother, at the onset of the coma, told Edwarda the she would never leave her. Hence, the title of the book. Edwarda has neither been on life-support nor even had a bedsore in all that time.

Because their home was located in Miami Gardens, Andy and I decided to extend our seminar trip and make an appointment to go visit with them.

Kaye, who was seventy-four at the time we met her, fed and turned Edwarda every two hours, twenty-four hours a day. She also bathed her, exercised her limbs, and took care of her hygiene needs. Edwarda was, at that time, in a stage-nine coma, which means she could come out of it any minute. She is aware of everything going on in the room; she's just not able to communicate. Kaye told us Edwarda is what is known as a "victim soul." This is someone who offers up their pain or discomfort for the benefit of humanity. That is **her** purpose for being on the planet.

Kaye claimed that the Blessed Virgin Mary visits a couple of times a week. I wasn't sure if I believed that, but I figured, *What the heck, it can't hurt to check it out. Pope John Paul and Mother Teresa had been able to see Mary. Who am I to judge?*

The day we were scheduled to visit Edwarda and Kaye, I had a migraine. On the way to our visit, I started to take a dose of migraine medicine. I don't like taking it because it knocks me out, but the migraine was bad. Just before I put it in my mouth, a feeling came over me that I should refrain from ingesting the medicine. Wanting to see what would happen, I didn't take it. However, the closer we got to the house, the worse I felt. The migraine was so bad, my stomach was getting upset.

When we walked in, Kaye greeted us like we were old, long-lost friends. She instructed me to go around to the other side of the bed and put Edwarda's hand into mine. My hands had become very chaffed because of the change in climate, and my scaly skin was starting to split. They were painful, like having paper cuts and getting lemon juice in the cuts. I was reluctant to touch Edwarda because of their roughness; so with my right hand, I just rubbed her shoulder where her gown covered her skin, which was as smooth as that of a baby. I remember Kaye telling me that I was standing where the Virgin usually stood.

Including Kaye and Edwarda, there were seven of us in the room. Andy, me, Donald (our friend and host for that stay in Key Largo), a young man that we recognized as a facilitator from the Tony Robbins seminar, and his cab driver.

We learned later that when the cab driver heard where his fare wanted to go, he told the young man that there would be no charge. The driver stayed the whole time and quietly prayed with his rosary in the corner.

Our visit lasted about forty-five minutes, during which time Kaye talked almost non-stop. She showed us an award bestowed upon her by Pope John Paul. It is the highest honor a Catholic can receive. She was so unassuming and didn't have a tooth in her head, but her crystal-blue eyes shown as though a bright light was beaming inside her soul. She was very upbeat and enthusiastic, happy to have us visitors, exhibiting a pep and energy that belied her age of seventy-four.

Kaye's eyes impressed me so—they were enormously alive! It felt as if they never left my face—as though I was the only person in the room.

When we got ready to leave, she asked us to pray with her. Extemporaneous prayer has always made me somewhat uncomfortable, but since she was doing all the praying, I went with the flow.

Kaye asked God to bless our expected granddaughter—although at that time, her gender was still unknown to us. Kaye mentioned our granddaughter was definitely going to be a very special child. I had not a clue at that time how accurate this prediction would be. She asked God to protect us on our trip home to St. Louis and also give us a smooth ride back to our friend Donald's house.

Afterwards, she also gave us a snapshot of a group picture taken in her front yard next to Mary's rose bush. She explained it was the Blessed Mother's rose bush because the roses were blue, Mary's favorite color. Neither the bush nor the roses had any thorns. Most impressive was the Virgin's silhouette, visible in the foreground of the picture.

Our ride back to Donald's house (headache and nausea free for me!) was made in almost half the time it would have normally taken. Donald, who had stayed near the door in Edwarda's room during our visit, kept commenting that he couldn't understand what was going on with the traffic. We were driving in the left lane, which was clear for at least a thousand feet in front of us. Even though the other three lanes looked like a parking lot. Oh, cars would pull in, but then pull right out again. As if someone was saying to the driver, "No, no, you don't want to be in this lane." Did I mention this was during five o'clock rush hour?

As we travelled along in this weird bubble of open road, naturally we talked about our experience with Kaye and Edwarda. We discussed how peaceful the room was, and that time seemed to stand still while we were there. Just then, Andy mentioned how he had the sense that Kaye was talking only to him, validating my very same sensation.

The next day, when the ticket agent at the airport saw that we were willing to pay extra to get home a few hours earlier, she asked, "Why the hurry?" We told her we were trying to beat the birth of our grandchild. She exclaimed, "*That* deserves the baby seats," as she upgraded us to first-class. We ate and drank like royalty all the way home, even topping off the trip with fresh-baked, chocolate-chip cookies (my favorite) and ice-cold milk.

The airport cab driver must have overheard Andy's conversation on his cell phone with our son-in-law that our daughter had been induced for labor, because we made the trip from the St. Louis airport all the way to St. Luke's Hospital in twelve minutes flat. Rebecca Marie made her debut into this world three hours later. Believe it or not, my chafed hands with split fingers were healed and smooth enough to hold her.

Today, that beautiful, mature, spirit-filled girl, **Becca**, is seventeen years old and a senior in high school. She is truly amazing. I don't think I've ever met a more even-tempered, unassuming, upbeat, and responsible young lady. She's an excellent student and athlete, with more awards, friends and teachers that admire her then any two teens I know. Small children are mesmerized by her, and parents instinctively know to trust her.

I relay this experience because I find it so hauntingly beautiful that to leave it out (as one of *so* many times in my life that I have been aware of God's presence) would be a great dis-service—to Him and to you!

We Meet A Spiritual Mentor
Fall 2001

In fall 2001, after bouncing from church to church for some time, we sort of landed on one not far from our home. The young priest was like a breath of fresh air. He really "rang my chines" (and Andy's as well) by following his homily every Sunday with a second one for the kids using puppets! We were mesmerized and like little kids ourselves, we made sure that we always had a front row seat.

We had gone to South Carolina in September for a nephew's wedding. That was when 9/11 happened, and everybody (and I do mean, EVERYBODY) was in church, even if they had never gone to church before in their lives. The groom's older brother (our other nephew, Eugene, who wasn't even Catholic) got up and went to Mass with us just because he wanted to be with family.

The church was packed. There was no place to sit, so Eugene and I were sitting on the floor with our backs against a pew. Andy had dropped us off before going to park the car. He hadn't made it inside the church yet, and I had no idea where he was. Everyone was so convinced the attacks just days earlier meant the world was coming to an end, and they had better get holy! While sitting there, I remember thinking, that if Eugene could get himself up to go to Mass just so that he could be with us, then I could certainly get myself up to go back to church on a regular basis.

My leaving our home parish after the priestly turnover had been difficult for me, especially given my acute awareness as to how God was working in my life. But at the time, I felt it was what I had to do.

I did keep in touch with many of my dear friends from St. Joseph's. Soon after returning from our South Carolina trip, while talking to the teen music director on the phone, our conversation turned to their new pastor, of whom I was unaware since I was busy "church hopping" trying to find a new fit. When she asked if I had met him yet, my answer was, "No . . . I've been playing the field, so to speak." She suggested that I give him a try—she thought I might like him.

The following weekend, Andy and I went back to St. Joe's to check out the new pastor. I was leery. He could be another wolf in sheep's clothing—you can't be too careful in these matters!

Long story short, I was impressed! Not only was he an excellent speaker, he held your attention—never failing to make it interesting. Often, depending on the talk, Father would throw some humor in there to keep us awake, even though that part wasn't necessary. I *loved* his humor. He didn't fill his allotted time with platitudes or talking down to us. Neither did he speak over our heads. He used everyday English, and he always left us with a message. And at the end of his homily, our daughter and I would invariably look at each other and give him two thumbs up behind his back!

In no time at all, Father Tom (as he liked to be called) began to feel as comfortable as a well-broken-in pair of old shoes. I can't think of anyone who became part of a community as fast as that man did. He was a "people person." He didn't care about business—he had paid staffers working for him to take care of that piece.

He also had an awesome memory, making it a point to learn peoples' names. He *always* greeted you by name, quickly becoming the heartbeat of the parish.

Around 2002, a personal friend from San Antonio had been telling Father Tom about a new format for a Catholic retreat that was taking San Antonio by storm. Referred to as "ACTS," it based its program in Adoration, Community, Theology and Service.

He invited St. Louis to come down for a visit and witness this new wave that was helping to cultivate enthusiasm in many parishes. Taking along some interested St. Joe's parishioners, Father Tom made a trip to Texas, curious about all the excitement.

The troupe came back rejuvenated and extremely inspired. Their ACTS retreat experience had been extraordinary, and they had laid down a plan for the San Antonio folks to come up here and help conduct a retreat on in our area. "Seed planting," they called it—showing us the way to get it implemented here in Missouri.

It just so happened that we already had access to a retreat center that was falling into disarray due to lack of use and finances. So, a bunch of St. Joe parishioners gave it a face lift using their own "sweat equity."

Hold Onto Your Hat!
2003

Andy attended the first men's ACTS retreat in our parish. Once you attend, you become part of the team for the next retreat.

When Andy came home from his first retreat, I could tell that he wanted to talk about it. It surely had affected him in a profound sense, but one of the stipulations is to keep your experience to yourself.

Since a river separates Manchester (where St. Joseph's is located) and the city of Eureka (where the retreat center is), they came up with a slogan. "What happens on this side of the river, stays on this side of the river." It soon got shortened to, "Remember the river rule." Confidentiality is essential and maintained because there are so many surprise aspects of the weekend, they don't want to spoil it for those not having yet attended.

Still licking my wounds from the fallout with Father Tom's predecessor, and totally involved in my prison work, I was in no hurry to jump into something new. The next women's retreat was coming up, and in spite of rave reviews, I was doing my best to try and avoid it. I didn't think I'd have trouble doing this since the retreats all seemed to be filling up quickly. On the other hand, I was beginning to feel somewhat guilty because I knew Andy was very turned on about this new thing and really wanted me to experience it, too.

About a week later, I got wind that seventeen women were already on the retreat waiting list. So, I figured I was safe to have Andy sign me up, being certain that I wouldn't have a chance. Next thing I know, the retreat director is calling me up to congratulate me on being part of the upcoming event!

At the time she called, I was (literally) going through the mail. And of all things, I found a court summons for me to do jury duty at the very same time as the retreat! Thank you, God!

So, I said, "Gee, I'm sorry, but I just found a jury summons in the mail. Maybe you should call the next gal on the list. I'll go next time."

Upon reporting for my jury obligation, I get picked for a case. We get to court only to find that these two couples (living next door to each other) had been fighting over a piece of property between them for two and a half years. However, believe it or not, after having made two trips to the court house in two days, they decided to settle in the judge's chambers. God can play hard ball when he wants his way.

I had promised to keep the retreat director apprised of what was going on and if my situation changed. Remembering the story of Kaye and Edwarda (*A Promise Is A Promise*), I did make the call, still certain that any openings would have surely been filled.

Imagine my perplexity when she said, "Oh, good! I knew you would be able to make it! So, I didn't call anyone else."

"But how could that be?" I asked her, "I heard there were seventeen women on the waiting list!"

"*There were*," she said, "But for whatever reason, seventeen women had to drop out!"

I honestly felt like I didn't need another retreat as we were so heavily involved with the prison ministry. However, "Someone" had other plans. As it turned out, *this* retreat was planned especially for me—by God. Yes, I had been on many retreats; and yes, on every one I grew emotionally and spiritually. After each retreat, I always felt a little different when I walked away—but, *this* one—THIS ONE changed me irrevocably. It literally left me a new person!

When I arrived at the retreat center, it didn't take me long to figure out that God had special plans for me. Actually it was the Virgin Mother. Much to my surprise, as we were very involved in one aspect of the weekend, I distinctly heard a woman's voice say to me, "*If you'll let me, I would love to be your Mom.*" She didn't say "Mother," she said "*Mom*"—and I knew it hadn't come from any woman in that room!

I became overwhelmed with emotion, and I started to weep. Even today, I well up every time I remember that incident. At the time of the episode, I was trying like crazy to suppress my reaction. I did not want to melt down into a sobbing fool in front of all these ladies. The more I tried to choke it back, the stronger it fought to come out. I was even trying to stuff tissues into my mouth to halt the feelings! But just as I stood to do my part of that particular exercise, the damn broke!

At that very moment, I **KNEW** that if I were to faint dead away right then and there, I would never hit the floor! That there were about sixty women in that room who would catch me! Which is pretty much what happened. Before I knew it, I was sitting down, surrounded by all the other participants. Someone had pulled up a chair for me right next to a therapist (purely coincidental, I'm sure). All the women around me were giving me tissues, handing me water, even patting my back.

Have you ever gone into the *ugly* cry? I mean so hard that you have trouble catching your breath? Every time I think about that experience, my eyes tear up. And that was fourteen years ago.

What I learned here was, oddly enough, that I didn't trust women. Looking back on it—when your mother knows that you are being sexually molested and still leaves you home alone with the perpetrator and even buys you see-through pajamas . . . hello? That's a clue.

Other than twelve-step programs, I didn't know anything about community. When you're in the middle of a melt-down, and you *know* that sixty women have your back, you've just been "welcomed" into the community!

My mother couldn't love me because she didn't love herself. She took on as her own all the shame and ugliness that my grandfather and father heaped on her. I don't have to do that! My mother's biggest fear was that someone would find out her secrets! It didn't matter what the secrets were, she was afraid of *everything*!

As for me, I'm finding that the more *open* I am, the more people trust me; and the more *I* learn to trust others.

I have come to realize that I **am** somebody. I've **always** been somebody. I have a purpose in life. I am living that purpose by sharing my brokenness, my healing, and my philosophies with others—pretty much daily in one fashion or another. And those with whom I share myself somehow start to believe in *them*selves. I have discovered I am very good at what I do because I draw on my life experiences. **God is the Power inside of me fueling my momentum**.

The Locksmith
2005

I should have known from the start that this was NOT going to be just a "vacation with the girls," which I don't do anyway. First of all, it started out peculiarly. Going to Europe had never even been on my radar; certainly not in the top ten thousand things I wanted to do on my bucket list.

But it seems that a crew of my new friends were going to Medjugorje, Bosnia. Medjugorje is a small town in what used to be called Yugoslavia prior to the war ten years earlier. It is a site like Lourdes or Fatima where it is said that the Virgin Mary, Jesus' mother, has made appearances. At Medjugorje, Mary first appeared to six young visionaries in 1981, and she has been returning on a regular basis ever since.

In the Catholic faith, although we don't *worship* the mother (as some people of other faiths frequently misconstrue), we do hold her in very high esteem. Because of her close ties to Jesus, many of us ask her in prayer to intercede on our behalf, especially when our requests have something to do with children and/or family issues. Countless miracles have been reported in Medjugorje, and many documentaries elaborate on Mary's appearances.

Just to give you an idea of where I was being invited to visit, the entire countryside exhibited the aftermath of the recently-waged war. Rusty, overturned military vehicles littered the landscape, huge craters remained scattered throughout, and trees had only just started new growth out the sides of sheared stumps. In the towns, bullet holes scarred everything you laid eyes on. Buildings were indiscriminately strafed—hospitals, churches and orphanages alike. Everywhere **EXCEPT** in Medjugorje, the little village where the six visionaries lived.

So, when I ran into "the girls" at a potluck dinner, I was not just being cavalier when I told them to have a good time. I wasn't interested in their invitation to go. It had never once occurred to me that a personal visit might be a powerful pilgrimage.

I will admit that after the ACTS retreat I attended with them through our church a few months earlier, I felt more healed. So much so, that I didn't feel the slightest twinge of, "Oh, my God, I'd better go if I want them to like me." Not that I didn't care if they liked me. But for the first time in my life, I felt more at home in my own skin. For the first time in my life, I *believed* I was loved and accepted by women—a community of women!

Inside the prison where I worked, I had learned to let the real *me* shine through. The men accepted and trusted me for myself.

But I had never felt accepted by, nor did I trust, women. Undoubtedly thanks to my *mother!*

However, my old people-pleasing tendency did rear its ugly little head when one of the women at the potluck table leveled me with an eye-locking glare as she softly asked, "Will you, at least, *pray* about it?"

Replying with a light, airy, "*Sure!*" I moved on.

Later, I told Andy about the incident but offered no other comment. Then, a few days later, I asked him if he had thought any more about going to Medjugorje.

"No, do you want me to?" he quipped.

Thoughts about the trip just wouldn't leave me alone. At odd times, frequently in the days that followed, the idea of going to Medjugorje would pop into my head. Finally, I decided to use our Day of Reflection at LaSalle Center as a day of discernment.

I still had this overwhelming feeling of not being worthy. It was okay to spend money on Andy, the kids, the grandkids, even the new condo to which we had recently downsized; but I wouldn't dream of spending anything on myself. It wasn't until someone suggested to me God would *never* think I was unworthy that I made the decision to tell

Andy about how thoughts of the trip had been nagging me. His reply was, "I think you're being called to go." That's when I gave in.

The whole business was so out of character for me. I wasn't crazy about traveling, especially traveling without Andy. To top it all off, I had been dealing for months with *plantars fasciitis*, an inflammation of tendons beneath both arches in my feet.

Then came the setback. I had gotten the time off from work, cleared my desk for the next two weeks, and even bought some new clothes. I was all but packed when I received the phone call. Andy couldn't find our safe deposit box key to get my passport. Interestingly enough, I didn't panic. I just knew that if I was supposed to go, I would. If he was supposed to find the key, he would.

My boss, however, had other ideas. She was excited for me about the trip and was determined to ensure I went, even if she had to bodily put me on the plane. It just so happened that her neighbor and best friend was to be my tour roommate. As I recall, my boss's exact words were, "*Why are you still here?*! Why aren't you at home helping Andy look for that key? Don't **make** me go to that bank! You're not peaceful; you're just subconsciously sabotaging this trip. You're doing everything you can to get out of going!"

She would have been right about all of that in the beginning of my journey to this excursion. But as I became committed to the plan,

I just relaxed into the process. Scheduling obstacles magically seemed to somehow melt away. God himself was clearing my calendar, or so it seemed—until that call came from Andy.

By evening, the key hadn't yet been found, but Andy had a plan. One of his friends was a retired bank president. Consulting with him on options, the friend advised Andy, "It takes about forty-eight hours to cut through all the red-tape and get a bank-appointed locksmith to open the box. BUT, if you walked in there with your own locksmith, you just might get them to open it on the spot."

So, at six-thirty on Saturday morning of Memorial Day weekend Andy armed himself with the phone and the Yellow Pages, letting his "fingers do the walking." Two, three, four tries—all he got were answering machines.

On the fifth call, it happened. The guy who answered the phone was leaving later that day to take his wife on a trip out of the country. He had only come in to the office for a couple of hours "to make a few extra bucks for the trip."

When Andy's call came in, he listened sympathetically to our plight. "Sorry, I can't help you," he began—then he stopped in mid-sentence. "But maybe I know someone who might—give me your number—I'll call you right back."

In the meantime, I had been planning to meet a friend and attend a meeting. Now I thought I had better change my plans and go the bank with Andy. Then I clearly heard a voice (not mine!) in my head say, "He needs to do this alone. He's the one who misplaced the key. He needs to mount his white horse and be your knight in shining armor again."

From this point, I will do my best to tell the story from Andy's perspective.

The locksmith calls back and tells Andy to meet his friend Jeff on the bank parking lot at nine AM. Jeff appeared at the appointed hour, driving an unmarked panel truck. He was a mountain of a man with unwashed, tangled hair trailing down into a billy-goat beard. He was sockless, wearing rumpled shorts and a slept-in tee-shirt. None of this exactly identified him as a "professional locksmith." He didn't look like *any* professional *anyone* had ever seen from **this** side of a prison fence. Andy's heart sank. He said a quick prayer, took a deep breath, and walked into the bank trying to look as if he hadn't a care in the world.

He introduced himself, and his "lock expert" to the female bank employee, who looked dubiously from Andy to the locksmith and back again before icily saying, "This is highly irregular . . ." Then suddenly, she stopped in mid-sentence, blinked as if a bit confused, and continued, "Come with me."

She led the two men into the vault where, Jeff the locksmith, worked diligently while Andy sat on the floor next to him and prayed. Even the bank lady was praying for us as she went about her work.

The longer Jeff worked, the more pungent he became.

At about the two-hour mark, Jeff grumbled, *"That does it!"* For the second time, Andy's heart sank. Knowing that Jeff had not yet cut through the lock, Andy assumed that the disheveled locksmith was going to fold up and depart. But instead, Jeff turned to Andy and said, *"Mister, I don't know where your wife is supposed to go, but **somebody** doesn't want her going. I have never had this much trouble in all my experience."* Then he turned to the bank employee and said, *"Ma'am, this door is coming off if I have to take out the whole wall."*

Fifteen minutes later, the lock was off. When Andy turned to the bank lady and asked her what he owed her for the lock (which Jeff had totally destroyed), she said, *"I think you've had quite enough trouble for one day—there will be no charge."* Jeff had done the deed with only fifteen minutes to spare before the bank closed for the long Memorial Day weekend.

With the trip starting out like this, I suspected I was in for quite a ride. Which I was! But that's another story.

Medjugorje
2005

When I arrived at the airport I was greeted with the words, "Open your suitcase. We need to get rid of these drugs—so everybody is going to have to take some!"

Are you kidding me? *We're* supposed to be the good guys! Isn't there a law against this? If they were illegal drugs, yes! But these are desperately-needed medical supplies that we are taking to a war-torn country.

"Oh, okay, *that's* different."

I was one of nineteen travelers in our group. A few of them had made this trip in the past. Our guide was there many times. Over the next ten days, she regaled us with stories of others who had experienced mini to major miracles, although I wonder if there is such a thing as a "*mini* miracle."

The trip for me was very challenging because of my plantar fasciitis which had been causing severe foot pain in both feet for the past several months. It literally was so bad that at one point during the trip over, I told some of my traveling companions to just leave me in the airport and pick me up on their way back to the states. I was willing to sit there by myself for ten days rather then walk on the marble and concrete airport floors any further. My roommate, who was a nurse, was so supportive that she gave me her Crocks (rubber sandals) to soften the blows on my feet. They helped, even though they were two sizes too big!

I wish I could remember more details of the trip, but it's as if someone "wiped" my mind. I know that when we went to Mass, the church was packed beyond capacity—even the standing room was maxed out. If you *were* lucky enough to get a seat, it was probably gone when you came back from communion. Mass was held continuously all day—in one language after another. Those waiting outside for the next Mass in their language would push their way in and grab any empty seat while communion was being served. Not really very Christian!

I *do* remember three experiences quite clearly. One, concerned Ivan (one of the six visionaries) meeting with Our Lady on Apparition Hill.

Several of us were separated from the larger group. Whenever we went somewhere, a few of the women would share a taxi to save on the walking, splitting the nominal cab fare. I was always in this group since I just couldn't walk any distance. The others were also in poor health or elderly.

This day, when we got to the base of the hill, one of the women thought it was too dark, too dangerous and simply *too* much.

Most of this smaller group agreed. Except one, who said that she was going to be exceedingly disappointed if she didn't get to go up Apparition Hill. I was pretty much agreeing with the women who wanted to go back to the hotel, but for some reason, I told her that I would go with her if it meant that much to her. So, the two of us "egged" each other all the way up the hill to two large boulders where we had a pretty good view of the spot below where Ivan was to actually meet with the Virgin Mary.

I remember that every dog within what seemed like a fifty-mile radius was barking as if each of their homes were being invaded. They went on and on for about ten minutes. Suddenly, the barking stopped completely, as if someone had suddenly turned the volume off!

We watched Ivan, who was speaking to someone we couldn't see. But we could *smell* a very fragrant aroma of roses. (Roses are said to be Mary's favorite flower.)

Ivan's gestures and mannerisms all indicated that he was in deep conversation with another person. He would stop periodically as if he was listening. After about ten or fifteen minutes, he turned to the huge crowd of people that were holding their collective breaths and repeated what was said between himself and the Virgin. And *all the while* we could smell this wonderful fragrance of roses.

Once the excitement was over, the crowd started the dangerous trek back down the hill, and the dogs resumed barking. But now it was sporadic, occasional barking—nothing like it was, prior to the visit.

Only then did we realize we hadn't thought about how we were going to get down from there! We had one flashlight between us, and nothing but a couple of walking sticks to help us with balance.

My partner asked me to hand her the flashlight. She shined it back up the hill, right into the eyes of her son and his friend who was a seminarian.[*]

The son asked his mother how she knew where to shine the flashlight. She replied, "I heard you very distinctly. You told me to be sure to put one foot down before you lift the other one."

He paused, looking at her quizzically before saying, "Mom, I haven't said a word since the apparition."

Coming *down* the hill is much more treacherous than going up. For one, it was dark and very hard to see. Second, when going up you step on the next boulder with the front of your foot. This actually felt

---

[*] A young man studying to become a Catholic priest

wonderful to my poor mistreated feet because it was stretching out the tendon, which eased the pain considerably.

Coming down, however, was a whole *'nother story*! The nearly constant pounding on my heels was incredibly painful! Fortunately, the two guys' stream of patter helped distract my attention, and before we knew it, we were on solid ground.

When we got back to our rooms, I thanked God for my nurse roommate. She gave me not one but *two* foot rubs as I was in such pain that I couldn't stop writhing. When she finished the first one, she went and found some lotion; and I fell asleep during the second round. From that point forward, my right foot started to ease up and, eventually, stopped hurting completely.

There is another experience that was so powerful I must share it with you. All throughout the trip, our tour guide relayed many, many stories of people who had come to Medjugorje with terrible deformities or ailments and became cured, one after the other. One morning while standing at the window in our room looking out, I asked God, "Why Lord? What's wrong with me? Am I chopped liver?"

Immediately, I heard *the* Woman's voice softly say, "My child, you're acting like a spoiled brat!"

I *knew* who that was, and I also knew she was 100% correct! My properly chastened response was, "So, sorry Mother, you're absolutely right! Thank you! I'm good!!"

And I *was* good! End of reprimand. Except that my left foot was still almost unbearable.

For my sake, a smaller group of the original nineteen waited until near the end of our visit to do the stations of the cross because it involved a great deal of climbing the hills where the stations are physically located. Most of our group had already made the trek earlier throughout the ten days, but a few came along again, wanting to see my reaction when I reached the top.

When I finally tackled the stations walk, we reached a point at the peak of a hill. One of the gals was looking up, her hand shielding her eyes on top of her sunglass frame. She would lift her glasses, squint, then drop her glasses back to her nose while saying, "Nope, not yet!"

But then—it happened! And I witnessed the most amazing thing I have ever seen! I looked into the sky and saw the sun actually *spinning*! First it would spin in one direction, then it would slow to a stop before turning to spin in the other direction. Then, it floated through the air like a bouncing ball, with vivid colors emitting all around the edges. I was filled with a keen sensation of awe, wonder, and gratitude—*overwhelming* gratitude.

That's when I learned that my fellow travelers had already seen the same remarkable thing happen the day before. They were just waiting to share it with me! Thank you, God, for allowing me to be a part of such an incredible experience!

ACTS Forgiveness Talk
2005

    Shortly after returning home from Medjugorje, we were in full swing for the upcoming ACTS retreat. Many of us women who took the trip were members of the retreat organizational team. My own main team assignments were in the capacity of table leader and to be one of the speakers for the "forgiveness" talk.

    I began my talk with the song *I Am A Voice* from the Divine Mercy Chaplet, and ended the talk with *The Power Inside of Me* from the movie *The Mirror Has Two Faces* with Barbra Streisand and Jeff Bridges (sung by Barbra Streisand and Brian Adams).

    During the talk, I told them pretty much what I've just shared with you in previous chapters. I've learned that forgiveness is letting go of one's "justified" feelings of resentment. It is *not* condoning whatever action caused the resentment. Nor, is it letting the perpetrator *off the hook*. Also, forgiveness is *not* about understanding. Understanding has to do with the <u>head</u>; forgiveness has to do with the <u>heart</u>. Forgiveness does *not* require forgetting, nor can you forgive that which *you yourself* have already forgotten! Forgiveness *inspires* change, rather than **waiting for it to happen**.

After my talk at the retreat, I left the room while the Streisand song was still playing. The participants had the lyrics in front of them. When I got out into the hall, Father Tom, grabbed me up in a bear hug, and swung me around. Then all the other team members were there, too—congratulating me. When the song ended, the room literally erupted. It was surreal.

Because the talk went a little long, we adjourned to the chapel from there. Those women were so revved up that I had trouble getting their attention to tell them that we were offering them the opportunity to go to confession and receive the sacrament of Reconciliation, after which another surprise would be celebrated. Typically, only a portion of the retreat participants would elect to participate in confession.

When I finished my instruction, I walked to the back of the chapel to talk to one of the other team members. Before I even got started, she said, "Oh, my God, turn around and look at this!"

It looked like a fire sale! Every woman in that room had a cross in her hand and was trying to get to a priest. Not one woman skipped Reconciliation. Some of them even came to me later during the weekend to report they hadn't been to confession in as long as thirty years until that day!

Once again, I got the clear understanding, without a doubt, that God was using me that weekend! I still feel very blessed and humbled by it. Just as I do every time I share my story at a twelve-step meeting or go into the prison.

As if that wasn't *enough* praise from God, later the same evening I stopped in to see my Medjugorje Apparition Hill climbing partner, who was also on the retreat team. She was going over her retreat talk which would be given the following morning. I wanted her to be the first to know that **my left foot had completely stopped hurting**! Apparently, God *was* pleased with me!

I'm The Director?
2009

In fall 2009, I received a call at work asking me if I would be willing to serve as director for the upcoming women's ACTS retreat. My first question was, "Are you sure you have the right Mary? You know there must be a million of us at St. Joe's?"

His answer was, "You are Mary Rachelski, right?"

"Yes."

"Then you're the one!" His next comment was, "You don't have to answer me right now—why don't you think it over and give me a call back?"

Whooaa! I did not see *this* coming! "Good idea," was my response.

The first thing I did was call Andy. When I told him about the request, he got all choked up. Then *I* got choked up. It's a great honor, but I don't think I've ever been more blindsided. I kept expecting someone to call back and tell me that they made a mistake.

I knew if I was going to accept the job, I would need our daughter, Stacy, as my co-director. When I told her about the request, she asked, "Are you going to do it?"

My answer was, "The only way is if you would be my co-director."

"Whooaa," she said.

I exclaimed, "That's *exactly* what *I* said!"

A good director is only as good as her co-director. Stacy is organized and responsible; and they don't call me "Squirrel" for nothing. As I said before, I'm a great sales person, but coordinating details is not my strong suit.

Well, she finally consented, but I don't think she'll ever do it again with me. Not that we would ever be invited to do it together again, unless I was *her* co-director. She has her own musketeers, for which I'm very grateful. And she's already been an ACTS co-director for both of them.

A director can get away with being a ditz, because she is more like an emcee. The co-director is the brains behind the operation. The reason I don't think Stacy would ever be my co-director again is because (as I told you before) I rely heavily on God. So, when Stacy would ask me if I wanted to do this or that now, my answer to her would usually be, "I don't know yet."

She would come back with, "What do you mean, you don't know yet?"

I'd say, "The Holy Spirit hasn't told me yet!"

I don't know how many times during our weekend Stacy would exclaim, "You're driving me crazy!" I'm sure after the retreat was over, she went home and climbed into a nice, hot bubble bath with a tall glass of wine. She deserved it, and she is over twenty-one. But for me, it was a lovely experience I will cherish always because I knew she had my back the whole time! She is *very* capable.

By the way, the weekend was awesome! But then I knew it would be, because I had two aces in the hole, Stacy and the Holy Spirit!

Help's On The Way
2009

After he retired from his sales job, Andy started working with our children (who had a construction company) as their project manager/coordinator. Now they were ready to close the construction company.

I had been working at the prison without my ex-boss, Dave, for six years, and it was starting to lose its luster. Oh, I still loved what I was doing, but it just wasn't the same—it had been a two-person job from the beginning in order to do it *right*.

So, in October 2009, Andy became *my assistant as a volunteer*. What a God-send! He is so much more computer literate than me, freeing me up to do other things. Most of all, I loved having him at my back, literally. It was almost like having "Davey" around again, only better!

In addition, all the guys knew that we were married, so we became a shining example of how we could live AND work together but still get along. We even started doing some evening group sharing sessions with the guys, and they were very receptive. For some, we were like the mother and father they never had. Several of the correctional officers even started calling us "Mom" and "Dad."

Retired
December 31, 2011

I loved what I was doing and would have continued until I was too old to work. However, there was one *big* down side to this whole system . . . the paperwork! It had begun to eat up the bulk of my hours until I no longer had time for the men. I wasn't doing what God made me to do! And the fun was slipping away!

Government paperwork was just too overwhelming, especially when they never even referred to it, but they still insisted it be completed. It was the one and only unpleasant part of the whole position; and the longer I stayed there, the more time it took to get it done. I get very frustrated when others expect someone else to do their work for them, and it felt like the people in Jefferson City above me on the management chain were doing just that.

After working my paying job for eight years following the nine years Dave and I had worked together, I was starting to show signs of wearing out, even *with* Andy's help.

Finally, one day about two years after Andy joined me, I was so frustrated that without thinking first, I told the warden I was considering retirement and asked if she was interested in having me back as a volunteer. Her answer was, "I'd be a fool not to accept that offer."

So I said, "Okay let's talk."

Thus, on December 31, 2011, I retired. But only after ascertaining permission from the new warden that I *would* be allowed to come back as a volunteer. For me, prison ministry work seems like a heaven-sent opportunity. Now, I only put in about four hours a week, and it's all working directly with the men. I couldn't be happier!

Every day I'm there, I get to work with someone who wants to better themselves. Often I'm privy to that critical moment when he discovers that his past is all in how he looks at it. I believe that an angel once touched me with that knowledge. And now I am blessed to *be* an "angel" for someone else. I get to be God's hands, feet and mouth, enabling another one of His children to make a paradigm shift. Plus, I'm able to share it with Andy, my husband and best friend. We still go back in every week to teach classes. Sometimes we'll be teaching a class together, and other times we may be teaching different classes in different rooms. In almost thirty years, neither of us has ever had a serious confrontation with an inmate.

Life is good!

What I've Learned In Prison

- There are no mistakes, only lessons.
- Incarcerated men and women are genius material—they just need someone to help them find the good in themselves.
- If you want a *real* high, do something for someone who can't repay you.
- Understand that it is better to give than to receive.
- There are no bad people, just bad upbringings.
- Everyone, yes *everyone*, is a child of God.
- We all deserve to be treated with respect.
- If we could get all those people (inmates) to learn that we are here to serve others, not to *use* others, they could change the world.
- The staff person that talks down to an inmate says more about themselves than the inmate.

Boys I Met Along The Way

Boys I Met Along The Way

There is not enough time left on my ticket to tell you about *all* the men Andy and I have met over the years. Nor is my memory as sharp as it used to be. But each of those men, **IS** somebody! As I have said before, they are smart and amazingly quick at learning new things. The problem-solving ideas they come up with are often rather unorthodox, proving they can think outside the box. They are creative, given the right incentive. With respect, you will have someone that will complete the job and do it right in a fraction of the time it would take you to do it yourself.

We have volunteered in a women's prison, but that happened before I felt accepted by the women on my retreat. In my experience, women are harder. I suspect it's because they've trusted too many men who have used and abused them, and now they don't trust enough to want to go there again.

My much more extensive interactions with male inmates provided me a large percentage of what I perceive as *authentic* relationships, whereby I somehow reached the core emotional being behind the man.

Since I can't tell you about everyone I've met in prison, I picked out about a dozen or so who made a lasting impact on us.

They will be presented in no particular order. Just know that, each one has had a profound influence on me. In order to protect their privacy, names have been changed.

Sammy

Sammy was his nickname. His real name was John Wayne Samuel. He was a great fan of John Wayne and was quite proud to have been named after the infamous actor.

By this time, we had done a couple of retreats at MECC (Missouri Eastern Correctional Center) outside of St. Louis. We were already corresponding back and forth with some inmates. About one hundred of them to be exact, in three prisons in both Missouri and Illinois. One day, I got a letter from someone asking me to talk to his "cellie." A cellie is a guy with whom you share your room (cell). You may or may not like him. That is something the two inmates must work out.

It just so happened that the man I got this letter from liked his cellie and was concerned about him. He knew that Sammy was a great guy but that, to the best of his knowledge, he had no relationship with God. So, he figured if Sammy went on the next retreat, it would help him to rectify the problem. What he wanted *me* to do was to invite Sammy to the retreat. He truly believed if Sammy met me, that would fix him.

I sent a letter back, saying that although I was flattered and truly understood his concerns about Sammy, I just didn't have that kind of power. Besides, I was not comfortable setting someone up in such a way.

During that same time, I was working with a young man who was into genealogy. He asked me if I could go to the library and gather some information for him because they didn't have it in the prison reference materials. I told him I knew someone who was also into genealogy, and I would try and get some pointers from her; but that I didn't really have a lot of time to spend in the library looking up information.

I had heard about an area bookstore that sold secondhand books. So, I looked this place up and gave them a call. A cordial young man answered the phone. As I was trying to explain my mission to him, he received another phone call and had to put me on hold.

When he came back on the line, he asked me why I didn't go to the library myself. I told him that I was doing a favor for a friend who couldn't get out, and library employees didn't have time to look up all the information he needed. His next question was, "Why is it your friend can't go to the library himself?"

I told him, "Because my friend is incarcerated, and they frown on them leaving the prison to go to the library."

He queried, "Doesn't the prison have a library?"

I explained further, "Yes, but not information he needs on genealogy."

With that, he received a second phone call and had to put me back on hold.

When he came back, I told him all I was interested in doing was finding a book about genealogy that I could donate to the prison library.

Next he came up with the strangest question, "*Why are you getting involved with those kind of people?*" And then, believe it or not, a third phone call came through, and again I was put on hold.

By this time, I was starting to get ticked off, not only because of the interruptions, but because of his impertinent behavior.

So, when he came back for the third time, I'll admit I was a little rude, and I asked him what business was it of his why or to whom I wanted to give books.

I could not believe his answer—"Because you can't trust *those people*!"

Now, I was really irate, "Why would you say such a thing?!"

"Because I've had experience with them."

"Really? And that gives you a right to tell me who I should associate with?!" And then he *really* knocked me for a loop.

He said, "*Because I was one of them.*"

Well that put things on a whole new footing. "No kidding," I said, "Where were you incarcerated?"

When he told me MECC—well, my anger just dissipated! I said to him, "Then you, of all people, should know how it feels to be discriminated against! When were you there?" And he gave me the dates.

Then he told me who his cellie was (I knew the man). He said he got along well with his cellie, but that his *best friend was John Wayne Samuel, whom everybody calls Sammy.*

At that point my ears really perked up, "How did you know Sammy I asked?"

"*He runs an organization at the prison called YAG. It stands for Youth Awareness Group. I tried to get into it, but my time on the inside was too short. I would have liked to have been involved in that program. I heard about it through my cellie. I was impressed with the guys who were connected with YAG because they took a lot of crap from the other guys in the yard.*" Unfortunately, the young man that I was talking to had to get back to work, so he had to go. But he did check on the book that I had called about and told me where I could find it.

Later that week, I went to the post office to pick up mail from our inmate correspondents. In the stack was another letter from a completely different inmate, telling me how excited he was about going on the upcoming retreat. He asked me *how he could go about getting his friend Sammy to go, too.*

Now, the whole business is becoming curious. When someone whose name I had never heard before came up three times in less than a week, I got the distinct feeling that God was trying to give me a message. So, I wrote back to Sammy's cellie, asking for Sammy's address. I told him that I would invite Sammy to go and mentioned the apparent coincidences in how his name had come up repeatedly. But I also told him I was perfectly willing to let it go if Sammy wasn't interested in the retreat.

Well, long story short, Sammy *did* go to the retreat. Oddly enough, the seating arrangements worked out (strictly by chance) so that we were both sitting at the front of the room to the left and right of the podium. This gave me a perfectly good view of watching Sammy's reaction throughout the entire weekend.

In the beginning, he was there in body only. He appeared to be slightly agitated, like he had something else to do, or someplace more pressing to be.

That is, until the priest for the weekend got up to give his talk. I don't remember much about what Father said, but it seemed to be almost as if Sammy was simply tolerating him until he finished his talk so he could make a break to get out of there. Out of the blue, the priest used some form of profanity—I don't remember the word he used—shit? damn? hell?—but when that expletive came out of Father's mouth, Sammy's head shot up like someone had slapped him! Without realizing it, the priest had just captured Sammy's attention in the palm of his hand. That one word changed Sammy's complete demeanor, and along with it, his opinion of what was going on in the room. This man (the priest) had suddenly become real and trustworthy by Sammy's standards. From that point on, Sammy was riveted to everything that was said for the remainder of the entire weekend.

I made a point of introducing myself to Sammy, telling him that I was the one who sent him the letter explaining how his name had come up three times in less than a week. In the letter, I had told him that my husband and I would be part of the team and that we would like to personally invite him to come and experience the retreat; but that if he didn't feel comfortable, I certainly understood and would not take offense.

Much to my surprise, Sammy invited Andy and me to have lunch with him in the prison chow hall. That overture initiated the beginning of a long and very tight friendship for the three of us. I had the distinct pleasure of getting to know Sammy on a completely different level.

In July 1994 when Andy and I decided to become "professional volunteers" and had to sever our previous inmate correspondence, I had no idea this would lead to my eventually getting Dave's job as the Institutional Activity Coordinator. I had no idea that our coming into the prison for an occasional weekend retreat was going to play into the biggest growth spurt of my personal life. Little did I know, at the time, that *God had big plans for me*!

One of the job facets Dave eventually turned over to me was to coordinate all the weekly sessions of the YAG (Youth Awareness Group) program. It was the *original* scared-straight program! Its purpose was to invite teenagers at risk into the prison for a day in order to have a selected group of inmates (Sammy included) tell them, in no uncertain terms, exactly what it was like to live in prison. It was an up-front preview of what they might expect should they continue leading their current lifestyles.

Most of these kids were sent by parole officers, school counselors, teachers and parents—adults who were ready to throw up their hands in despair because they didn't know how to get through to the teens. I look back on those years, and I'm in awe as to how blessed I was to be able to spend time with this hand-selected group of men who volunteered their service to try and help young people see that they needed to make a course correction as to where they were heading.

That was over twenty years ago. I met so many young men like Sammy that I would've been proud to have as neighbors and friends, whom most of the world would shy away from because they wore a seven-digit number on their chest.

I never really found out what crime led to Sammy's incarceration—why he had a thirty-one year sentence. I never looked it up to find out because I didn't want it to get in the way of the work that we did together. More importantly, it wasn't any of my business, and he was no longer the man who did the crime that got him put into prison in the first place.

One day, Sammy (under his own volition) told me that the reason he was there was because he killed his wife. When it happened, he had recently returned from Vietnam, was suffering from PTSD, and before he realized what happened, she was dead at his feet. She was the daughter of a judge. I never checked it out, nor did I care, because this was one of the gentlest men I had ever met. I found it difficult to believe that he could do such a thing.

There were roughly twenty men involved in the YAG program at any given time. If one was asked to leave, or transferred, or went home, there was always another waiting in the wings to take over. They each had their own part to play during the five-hour program that they put on each week for these teenagers. As the "staff person in custody" for the YAG program, I felt privileged to sit in on these sessions.

What really impressed me with the group integrity was that each month, they would have what was called a "preach off." This meant if one guy felt that he could out-perform a segment of the program better than someone else, they would each do it in their practice sessions and then everyone would vote as to which man did the better job. This also included Sammy. The "preach offs" kept everyone on their toes and ensured the material was always fresh. The YAG team was constantly looking for new ways to keep the teenagers' attention.

One of the guys, Drew, even went so far as to take a memory course so that he could remember teenagers' names while they were there. He would use it in his spiel as a technique to keep their attention, calling a teen by name and asking him or her a question to keep them from becoming bored. Since most people crave attention, particularly teens, they tend to act out as a way of getting it. Calling them by name makes them feel important. The kids would always lag behind to ask Drew how he was able to remember all their names. His answer was always the same, "It's not important HOW I do it. What matters is that *YOU* are important enough for me to remember."

One required element for everyone on the YAG team was that they had to "walk the talk." If they got written up for any kind of prison rule infraction, they were suspended from the team. If the write-up stuck, and they were found guilty, they had to leave the group permanently. This was particularly difficult because team members were constantly being barraged by other inmates specifically trying to make them angry so they would be thrown off the team. Most of these provocations were born from jealously. Inmates are a lot like little kids in big men's bodies. The YAG team members built incredible character with scads of patience and tolerance as the result of this rule.

One YAG session touched me particularly profoundly. It was Sammy's turn to present, and he was talking about how the young people's actions affected *everybody*, but most especially their parents. He said, "Your parents love you, even though you may not believe it. Your being *here* today hurts and scares them, because they're so afraid you're going to live here someday."

Then this little voice in the front row piped up, "Nobody loves *me*."

Sammy stopped dead in his tracks! He stood in front of the young girl for the longest time, and then softly questioned, "Nobody loves you? Not even your mom?"

"No!" she spat out.

Sammy continued to stand there and look at her for a very long time, and I noticed tears were rolling down his face. Finally, he said,

"I will remember your face until my dying day." Then he walked to the back of the room and wept.

Another thing I remember about Sammy is that he loved animals. He once sent Andy and me an anniversary card he had personally made for us. He glued little pieces of different colored yarns inside (called fuzzy worms) with uplifting words in the message that he and Odie (the dog on the card) were sending us to remind us to share God's love. And inside he had a picture of himself holding four little kittens that had somehow wandered inside the perimeter of the camp fence.

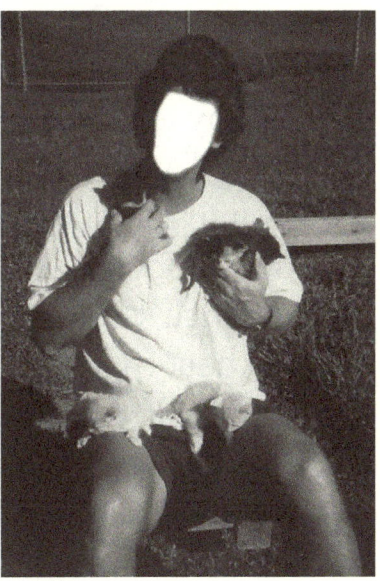

The night before Sammy was released from prison, Andy and I got permission to spend time alone talking with him in the chapel before he went home the next day. His entire family was forming a caravan all the way from Kansas City to come get him. Naturally, he was excited, but after thirty-one years of being locked up, he was also nervous and scared. He told us that one of the things he'd always wanted was a red Jeep. And when he got a job and saved up enough money, he was going to buy himself that red Jeep.

If there are enough jobs to go around, each of the inmates has an assignment. In Sammy's case, the YAG sessions were not only an assignment, they were a vocation. He also created another vocation for himself by learning to type braille. At MECC we had a program called "Talking Tapes." Inmates received a small monthly stipend for reading books into recorders, and in Sammy's case, he transcribed books into braille. He took one young blind man all the way through elementary school, high school and college, even transcribing calculus into braille.

About two years after Sammy was released, we got word that he had been killed in an auto accident. While driving on the highway in the rain, someone lost control of their car and ran into Sammy in his red Jeep. He was killed instantly.

The only sense I could make of his death is that he must have completed his mission on the planet. He was able to assist that young blind man all the way through graduation. Fittingly enough, when the "Talking Tapes" program was closed a few years later, God helped us to locate that young man and give him the braille typewriter.

Undisputedly, Sammy touched a lot of people while he was in prison. The letters came in on a weekly basis from YAG kids "who got it" and went on to change their lives for the better. I know there were many inmates who learned to *walk the talk* so that they could work with teens at risk. I also know they all have Sammy to thank for it. I learned so much for having known this man, and I believe some of what I do today is the result of his lessons. Hopefully, it makes me a better person, too!

Robert

Robert was one of the two clerks already working with Dave when I joined the inmate activity group. He was a man one would call an "old head" in prison terms. Meaning that he had a fair amount of time served already under his belt. He was gruff and mostly a no-nonsense kind of guy. A lot of people were scared of him—until they got used to his personality. A very responsible and dependable fellow, Robert did his job well. Dave relied heavily on him to get the work done, and Robert was not the kind of man to let you down. When he understood that you believed in him, he did everything in his power to come through for you.

Charles

Charles, the other inmate activities clerk was better known as "Chinchilla." Don't ask me why, I have no idea how he got the nickname, but I do know that a great many inmates prefer to go by a nickname of choice.

Charles and Robert made a great salt and pepper team. Robert was a large Caucasian man by stature but not overweight. While Chinchilla was a slightly-built African-American. Apparently, they had been working together for some time, and no doubt they were well suited for each other.

I do have one funny memory about Chinchilla that gives you a better idea of his personality. One day I arrived at the access point into our office area and rang the buzzer to enter. I was standing in the hallway outside of a door with a three-foot-square shatterproof window in it so that we could see who was pushing the doorbell.

When he realized it was me, Chinchilla pushed the latch-release button on his side to allow me access. A long conference room stretched between us. I stepped into the conference room and slipped out of sight to Chinchilla behind a file cabinet, waiting for him to look up and wonder what happened to me. Before long, I got a chance to sneak up to the next cabinet. On the third try, he caught sight of me, and the game was on! He let out a laugh like a kid at Christmas! What my little prank showed him was that I was not the enemy. Oh, yes, I represented staff, but I was definitely approachable.

Often, we get some officers in who lack self-confidence. These individuals like to heckle the men to somehow make themselves feel better. Kind of like poking a dog in the eye with a stick—sooner or later the dog is going to get even, and you're *not* going to win the dog over in the process. I know that little game of hide and seek meant a lot to Charles, because he mentioned it often with amusement. But most of all, I believe it had let him know that I was "safe."

Most of these guys are small children locked up in wounded men's bodies. I have heard so many of their stories over the years, and it's all I can do to keep from crying. If their lives growing up had been easier, most of them would probably be different people. What I strive to do when I am with them is ALWAYS treat them with dignity and respect.

Often when I'm inside a corrections facility, I actually forget I am in a prison. Certainly the prison administration would have had a fit if they knew that. But they recognize that I get so caught up in the men that I don't judge them. Not only is it not my place to judge, I don't even have the *inclination* to judge!

I feel closer to God in prison than I do at church. Being in there helps me to understand God better. I *feel* Him there. Just as I feel closer to God when I *see* Him through my husband, Andy.

I mentioned earlier that we started a twelve-step program in the prison. In the beginning, it was pitiful. Basically, me and two men. But God had big plans for that meeting. We called it "self-help," but before we knew it, it had grown so large that we had to come up with another day and then split the meeting into two groups. And these meetings fostered another venue for trust and acceptance—traits badly needing development by nearly every inmate in the facility.

Ted

One Friday morning, I came in ready with an outside speaker for the twelve-step meeting, and one of the regulars was standing in front of the meeting room doors with his arms folded over his chest. As if he wasn't going to allow me to enter. I asked him what was going on, and he said, "*I need to talk to you.*"

"Now?" was my question to him.

"*Now!*" came his reply.

"Well, okay then, let me get the meeting started and introduce the speaker, and we can sit out here and talk while the speaker is on—will that work?" That seemed to satisfy him, so I asked one of the guys to take over once the speaker was finished. Turning to Ted, I said, "Okay. You've got fifteen minutes to tell me what's going on, please."

It seemed that his wife was writing and telling him in great detail what she and her new boyfriend were doing in his hot tub. My heart just broke for him! I've heard it said, "Hell has no fury like a woman scorned," but this took the cake!

Ted actually started what became my pro-bono therapy business, because Ted became my first client. And I hadn't even graduated collage for psychology yet!

Ted's need to talk that day started what probably became at least a year-long session, pretty much daily. Any day I was there, Ted was with me in the conference room pouring out his heart.

Dave, my boss, had a very big heart and was fine with Ted's ranting and raving to me every morning. Thankfully, Ted was okay with venting his frustration in front of a well-trafficked office. He had a very colorful vocabulary, and I often thanked God for giving me a river-boat-captain grandfather who talked like a drunken sailor. I had heard almost all of the expletives, and I even used some of them myself once in a while.

What *was* apparent was that Ted was healing with these sessions. Because at the end of the year, I asked the guys in the twelve-step meeting whom they thought had helped them grow the most in the last year (thinking they would vote *me*). Instead, they voted Ted as number one! No one was more surprised than Ted. And no one was more *pleased* than me!

As a matter of fact, at one point, Andy and I had to go to California. I was afraid of what Ted would do if he got a letter he couldn't handle alone while we were gone. So, I took him down to the camp shrink, and made him promise to go see him if that should happen. He didn't need to go. Fortunate, being as Ted scared the hell out of the camp shrink.

Upon our return from the west coast trip, I found out that one of the younger, more childish inmates was in the kitchen bugging Ted one day; and instead of seriously harming the little guy, Ted just backhanded him and knocked him across a steam table. Don't believe I mentioned that Ted was one of the lead cooks in the kitchen and worked with knives all the time.

As a footnote, I was talking to one of the wardens about Ted after he was released. Upon telling her about the situation I just relayed to you, she gave me his phone number and allowed me to call and talk to him. Once they are released and off "paper" (meaning off parole), we can associate with them at will. They've served their time. They are free men and women.

It was wonderful! Ted was very excited to hear that I called and because he was driving at the time of my call, he called me back a short while later. We were both crying. He said he always wanted to talk to me but didn't know how to reach me. He said that I saved his life. Doing this kind of work doesn't get much better than that!

My Little Buddy – Danny

One of the two guys that helped start the twelve-step meeting with me was Daniel, more commonly known as Danny. He was a cool guy, one of those that makes you want to ask, "How in the hell did you ever get into prison?" Very intelligent, kind, soft-spoken and level-headed, he always went out of his way to be gentle and helpful with others. As matter of fact, he was a tutor at the prison school and became my best buddy! Small in stature, Danny sort of looked like he was still a kid, but he was a BIG man with heart and was well-liked by everyone.

When I was working at MECC, grants were available for the men to get a college education. Danny had always wanted to be a therapist. He was working on that degree, and at the same time was helping others work on *their* education. In a way, he was a cheerleader. He would talk at length with others to try and help them understand their gifts—insisting they had more to offer the world than they were currently sharing with others.

I'm sorry to say that I don't remember much else about Danny other then what I just told you. Except, that he finished his degree. And he did his fair share of therapist work (under the radar so to speak), with the inmate population before he was released.

We had "shrinks," as the men preferred to call them, working at the prison; but they seemed to leave a lot to be desired. You might have picked up on this when I told you about taking Ted down to meet one of them before we left for California.

Danny had a job driving a truck for a food company after being released. Knowing how Danny helped a lot of the inmate population is the only thing that helps me make sense of the fact that we lost him the same way we lost Sammy. The only difference I can discern is that Danny fathered a little girl before he was killed in an auto accident. Will she be able to carry on his legacy? And, if so, what is that legacy?

After having the privilege of knowing Danny and Sammy the way I did, I truly believe that God has a mission for each of us . . . and after we've completed our mission, He calls us home. Their missions were to be fulfilled, for the most part, while in that prison. But it still hurts like crazy for those of us left behind.

God's Grace – Keith

Occasionally God sends me a wonderful gift! One time we were at Epcot Center at Disney World waiting in line to go on a ride and I hear someone calling, "Mary . . . Mary . . . Mary."

I turned around and saw this guy leaping over the queue bars like he was O.J. Simpson. As he got closer, I realized that he's got his sights on me. And I started backing up. But he was fast, and then I hear him say, "Mary, it's *me, Keith*!"

It was another former inmate. When he was in prison, Keith had dreadlocks. Now his hair was close cropped. No wonder I didn't recognize him!

To see these guys out on the streets, joyful and healthy, is totally AWESOME! How appropriate to run into Keith at the "happiest place on earth."

Drew

And then there was the time I was in a store shopping when I notice this guy talking on his cell phone. I see that if he keeps going on the path he's taking, we are going to be on a collision course. So, I moved aside, and he did too, so we were *still* going to collide. Again I changed, and so did he. I was starting to get annoyed, grumbling to myself, *these people talking on the phone not paying any attention to where they are going are a pain.*

Suddenly, he shut his phone and grabbed me! I took a deep breath to scream, when he blurts out, "Mary, has it been so long that you don't recognize me?!" It was Drew, the guy that took the memory course so he could remember the kids' names at the Youth Awareness prison sessions.

The thing that amazes me most when I run into one of my "boys" on the outside is how happy they always look! Clean cut and proud! They walk taller and actually appear to be *bigger* men than they were in prison.

It makes me weep with delight every time I happen to run into one of them.

Orlando

Orlando, known as "O," actually spent more time with Andy than he did with me. He was in one of Andy's classes and became so impressed with Andy and the program that he re-took the class—five or six times as I remember.

Because Orlando was so familiar with the material, Andy made him an inside facilitator. He was good, too! He became a translator for the men. Quite often the guys are so used to speaking in prison jargon, or Ebonics, that they don't always understand English when conversing with a Caucasian

"O" turned out to be a man of principles—and a very skilled teacher! He learned quickly and had an interesting way of explaining the material to the guys which kept their attention. He proved to be a great asset and helped countless inmates in the time he worked for us.

He, too, is now a free man, enjoying life on the outside with a new and improved perspective.

Randy

Randy wasn't an inmate, at least not on my watch. I met him when he applied to become a volunteer and bring a twelve-step meeting into the prison. Yes, he had done some time, but not the amount of time our guys were serving.

Randy has an impressive plan, an idea that I hope he can make work because it has such tremendous merit. So many people could benefit from this project. He is in the process of starting a program whereby his organization will buy blighted houses and hire inmates just getting out of prison to learn how to rehab these houses.

The benefits are three-fold. Giving the inmate a job, teaching him a new trade, and helping rejuvenate neighborhoods. It's a win-win all the way around.

Sure, the plan has some bugs to work out, but the concept is brilliant, and I hope one day to hear that Randy has succeeded in his venture.

Impress Me! – Ron[*]

Ron turned his chair so that it faced me, sat down, kicked it back on two legs and folded his arms over his chest. "*Impress me!*" he said with a sneer.

I shot back with, "*I'm not here to impress you. But, if you think you can stick it out for the whole weekend, I guarantee, you'll be impressed.*"

I was one of a group of twenty-five volunteers to bring a three-day retreat into a prison where Ron was an inmate. That was in October of 1993.

Lucky for me Ron appreciated a good challenge and took me at my word. He got into the atmosphere and camaraderie. Before long, everyone at the table was getting to know one another. As much as I tried not to fall back into my old habit of sarcasm, it just came naturally. He reminded me so much of my younger brother. By the end of the three days, he was crying in my arms.

The universal tactic for inmates whether showing contempt or camaraderie is sarcasm, banter and friendly putdowns, all of which

---

[*] This story was published in *Chicken Soup for the Prisoner's Soul* ©2000

Ron was a master. His sharp tongue wielded quick retaliation—his victim was often unaware of the attack until later. His winning smile could dazzle and distract even the most cautious potential victim.

As the weekend progressed, a strange thing happened. Ron's sharp tongue started to relax. He took time with the slower inmates and showed incredible patience. He had natural leadership ability. It almost seemed as if he had been on this weekend before.

Ron's ability to coax even the most timid into opening up was amazing. He treated each person with respect, and his enthusiasm was infectious. Everyone began to look at Ron a little differently—including Ron. It was as if his conflict within had been replaced with an overwhelming eagerness to help others.

Although the team members and candidates represented a diverse group of religions, this Catholic-based program ends with a Mass. Ron made a point of sitting next to me during Mass. He peppered me with questions about the many changes in the Catholic Church during his twenty-two-year absence. He wanted me to help him brush up on his church etiquette, asking me questions like, *"Do we still take communion on the tongue? Do you think God would mind if I go to communion without having gone to confession first?"*

That macho facade was slipping away and suddenly he was a small child. He wanted to please God. That's why he was weeping in my arms. He told me that a drunken driver had killed his mother in a gruesome auto accident. The last time he set foot in church was to attend his mom's funeral. He was angry. And, he blamed God for her death. His mother was the mainstay of the family. After her death, they fell apart and went their separate ways. He hadn't experienced unconditional love since then—until this three-day weekend.

That was the beginning of Ron's growth. He went through the Breaking Barriers program at the prison. A program designed to help people discover the obstacles to their growth. When it came time for Ron to share, he told us of his dream of someday being reunited with his children. He painted such vivid pictures that we could almost smell his daughter's freshly washed hair as he brushed it in the sunlight. Every loving detail brought tears to our eyes.

Ron was using his natural leadership skills to help others. He had a newfound sense of pride in himself, and it showed. Everyone noticed the change in him, including his caseworker.

We tapped his thirst for knowledge when he eagerly agreed to help us establish a motivational library at the prison. He volunteered long hours setting up and cataloging all the donated books. He was like a kid at Christmas when a new shipment of material came in. He showed me how to type cards, bind books and gently break their binding so they could withstand years of use. We practically had to throw

Ron out of the office at the end of the day, so we could go home. He never thought of it as work because he was doing it for others. One of his perks was getting first choice at the new material. Because of his insatiable appetite for knowledge, he became the perfect choice to run the library.

Ron was transferred to another camp to complete a required program to qualify for parole. Then Ron was a free man, but he actually became free on that Friday afternoon in October of 1993.

God Works In Mysterious Ways – Richard[*]

    I looked across the room and my heart froze! There, standing among the other inmates lined up against the wall, was a younger version of my recently deceased father. It was so uncanny that even my husband, Andy, who was standing next to me, leaned down and said, *"Do you see that guy across the room? He looks so much like your dad, it's creepy."*

    Outwardly, I'm sure I looked calm and composed, but inside I was shaking. *Get ahold of yourself, I reasoned. It's probably just a trick of the lights. Maybe Dad's been on your subconscious mind; after all, it hasn't been that long since his death.*

    My childhood left much to be desired. My father and I had a talk years before his death during which we both agreed, he was not the father either of us would have liked. He had even given me the gift of an apology. Yet somehow, I still had the feeling that there had been no closure before his death.

---

[*] This story was published in *Chicken Soup for the Prisoner's Soul* ©2000

How do I get myself into these fixes? Here I was committing to bring a weekend retreat into this prison with my husband and twenty-five other volunteers. *Get a grip,* I kept telling myself. Finally, I decided just to avoid the man all weekend. *I can do that; it's a big room, lots of people. No problem! What's the worst that can happen? I'm here now. Just keep plenty of space between you, and you'll be fine.*

I was snapped out of my mental argument when I heard my name called. "The outside leader of table six, Mary Rachelski. First candidate sitting to her left, Richard." I managed to weave my way to the table, trying not to make eye contact with him. I reasoned, *If I don't look at him, he can't see me.*

"Hello, my name is Richard." I turned to look into the watery gray-blue eyes of the younger version of my father.

This man not only looked like my father, but he sounded like him, same mannerisms, same way of combing his hair, same big words used out of context like my father. He even wore the same after-shave. God has a cruel sense of humor, doesn't he?

Or does he? This man was like my father in almost every way, except that instead of making me feel stupid when I said something, he acted like I was the most brilliant woman on the planet! He validated everything I said and did. He laughed at my jokes. He got my snacks. He held my chair, and most of all, he never once made me feel ashamed. Now, after the initial shock, I could see that he wasn't exactly like my father, but I had to admit that the similarities were uncanny.

One of the most important and beautiful exercises of the weekend is the foot washing. We reenact the foot washing before the Last Supper in the Bible. It's an immensely powerful experience, because everyone is totally connected emotionally. You may see a white man washing a black man's feet or a man washing a woman's feet. Everyone humbles himself or herself.

I had just taken the place of someone who had been kneeling on the floor washing the feet of others, when I looked up to see the next person to sit down. You guessed it; it was Richard. Except this time, it wasn't Richard, it was my father. I started to cry. I was truly washing my father's feet with my tears. This was my chance to tell him I love him; I forgive him; and to go in peace. When I looked up again he was crying too, but he also had such a look of pure peace on his face. Then just as quickly, it was Richard again.

I couldn't wait to tell Andy what had happened on the way home. I wasn't sure if I was losing my mind. That night I couldn't sleep, so I wrote Richard a long letter, telling him all about my childhood and just what had happened that evening, and why it probably seemed to him that I must have been acting strangely that weekend. Only then was I able to sleep.

The next morning, I received clearance from the chaplain to give Richard the letter, and to my surprise he had spent several hours writing me a letter. He asked that I wait until I returned home to read it. This in part, is what it said:

> *Dear Mary,*
> *I almost didn't go through with the foot-washing exercise. You see, I didn't feel worthy. So before sitting down, I asked God for a sign to show me that he could forgive me for all the terrible things I've done in my life, many of which I've shared with you in this letter. I've only told one other person in this world my secrets. When I looked down into your face, you were crying. I thought that was my sign, and then I saw your face change, to that of Christ's.*
> *The Peace of the Lord be with you,*
> *Richard*

Walt

The last young man I want to tell you about is Walt. When Walt came into the system, he was seventeen years old. He was in every class that I taught, and his hand was always up, "*Miss Mary, Miss Mary—I know the answer, I know the answer!*"

And I would usually say, "Yes, Walt, I know you know, but let's see if anyone else knows." The other guys hated him, but Walt didn't care. He was going to make something of himself.

When he was ready to be released, he had set his sights on getting a job in a Fortune 500 company.

So, he went on an interview with just such a company. When the application asked him to check the box if he had ever had a felony, he wrote, "Will discuss on the interview." During his interview, after he was asked the same question, he was told that the firm didn't hire ex-cons. Walt thanked them and said, "Okay, I'll see you tomorrow."

In the meantime, Walt got a job working nights delivering newspapers. Each morning when he got off his delivery shift, he would stop in to the company on which he had set his sights and ask the same question, "Got any openings yet?" It reached the stage that when he stuck his head in the door to ask the question, the entire office staff would respond, without even lifting their heads from their work, in a collective voice, shouting, "***We don't hire ex-cons!***"

Then one morning, three guys had walked off the job the night before, leaving the boss in a very tight spot! When Walt stuck his head in the door, the boss asked, "When can you start?"

Walt answered, "How about now?" After working all night, he jumped right in and gave it everything he had! That was eleven years, and four promotions ago.

When God knows that you're determined, and you're doing the right thing for the right reason, he'll open doors for you! I want to add that Walt is working full-time at that Fortune 500 company and helping his wife raise their family, He also goes to school at night, working for a degree to better himself; AND he goes back into the prison to do volunteer work with the inmates. Who better to show them the way to get out and stay out, than someone who's *been there, done that*?

DOC Puts The "Fun" In Dys*fun*ctional

Prison Worker Perspective

Having been involved in the penal system for almost thirty years, I have had the unique experience of observing the system from two positions—volunteer and employee.

In general, the volunteers are not regarded highly by the employees, especially the custody staff. We're thought of as "bleeding heart liberals" or "scabs." The really sad part is that most of custody (or security as they are known by the general public) does not understand that volunteers are there to help, not hinder. Often, a volunteer can diffuse a volatile situation, whereas some custody employees make the same situation worse because they feel a need to show power.

Speaking of power, the sitting U.S. president is allowed to determine the name by which the men in prison are referred. For example, when Jimmy Carter was in office, he elected to use "residents," which he believed (and I agree) sounds less judgmental. Less like a negative label. I believe it was Bill Clinton who changed it to "offenders." That, to me, sounds like a constant dig, like they will never change. But as state employees, we were required to use the word "offenders" when referring to the prisoners. That terminology will stay in place until another president changes it.

Granted, most offenders often look at custody as "the police," someone just trying to catch them doing wrong. And, believe me, some of them are just that! These officers are often young and/or inexperienced. Other times they may be older and burned out. Either way, that approach can be dangerous.

The inmate on the other hand, may be young and foolish, trying to posture for his "homies." Or, perhaps he is a hardened criminal tired of being pushed around by over-zealous officers. Sometimes all it takes is the uniform. Or lack, thereof!

In my case, I believe that when I go "inside," I am automatically accompanied by Grace. Now, don't get me wrong and think that I walk in like some hotshot in charge.

I just know where I am. I am *not* acquainted with each man, his background, or how he is going to react; so I don't give them reason to feel threatened. I address them by their first name, if I know it, or "Dude," if I don't. It sounds less formal than using their last names. I am careful not to let my guard down. I've learned that a smile can go a *long* way. I'd rather give a guy the benefit of the doubt, than hang him out to dry if there is any possibility of his innocence on the particular situation.

Remember, I told you that I grew up with four brothers? Some lessons are learned early and are deeply ingrained.

I remember on one occasion when my reaction was purely instinctual—and I still think I did the right thing. I was standing in the conference room, just outside the door to the other office. A young inmate was standing just inside that office with the door open between us, and the light was off. What he was doing there, I have no idea, but technically he was out of bounds.

My boss was in our office just next to the office occupied by the inmate, and I could be seen by my boss.

All of a sudden, the inmate reached out to grab my hand. Without thinking, I yelled, "No!" and jumped back. In less than a heartbeat, my boss was out of his chair, around the desk and at my side.

Now my boss was a big man. He would have easily been able to take that young offender apart. He was also well-trained as he rose up the employment ranks from security to Institute Activities Coordinator. But there was no need for action. The kid himself jumped back and immediately started sputtering that he wasn't going to do anything. Dave growled at him, "I know you weren't—now get out of here and don't come back unless your intentions are good and honorable." Dave could have made a case of the incident and had the boy sent to "the hole," but he made a judgment call, and we never had any trouble with the young man again.

I've never encountered a serious confrontation with an inmate. However, I have had differences of opinion from time to time. I am never too proud to apologize for my part in a situation when appropriate. It almost always ends with a return apology.

This behavior lends itself well to my belief that I'm there to teach them the Golden Rule—*Treat others as you would want to be treated in return.*

Department of Corrections VS Delancey Street Foundation
How Delancey Got Started

Delancey Street was founded using a San Francisco apartment complex by Mimi Silbert and her husband in 1971 with four people and a $1,000 loan.

They had a set of twin boys and a dream—***an alternative to prison***. Mimi's husband has since passed away, but she still keeps it running. They now have five other locations nationwide. The mother house is in San Francisco, with spin-offs in Los Angeles, North Carolina, South Carolina, New Mexico and New York.

Each is a 501 (c) (3) charity under the federal law.

Perhaps, after reading this, you may be inspired to support them with a tax-deductible donation.

We Saw For Ourselves
2002

In autumn 2002, Andy and I had an opportunity to visit the Delancey Street facility in San Francisco for a few days. We stayed in a hotel close by, but spent our days at the location, partaking in the facility as if we were new arrivals. We wanted to get to know, first hand, what it was like to be a "new fish" in this system. I was certain it was nothing like being a "new fish" in DOC. And sure enough, it wasn't!

The first thing I want to tell you is that the gates to Delancey Street lock from the inside. You *cannot* walk in from the street. However, the residents can walk *out* anytime they want. They agree to a stay of two years, and most stay for four years. They are told ahead of time that if they decide to walk out before the end of the contract, their parole officer will be notified.

The 400,000 square foot, city-block-long, four-storied building was totally built by the residents. Five hundred of them inhabit the upper floors, while the street level showcases retail storefronts run by the residents. All of it was designed by Mimi Silbert.

As a new resident, I was assigned first to the laundry. Another girl, much younger, was chosen to "break me in." She had only arrived the day before, but was able to explain to me not just *how* the job was done but also *why*. Delancey's philosophy and motto is, *Each One Teach One*.

There are no supervisors. That's right, **no one is superior over another**. The more experienced resident shares knowledge with the newer one. **There are no paid staff personnel**.

I really liked the fact that they explain *why* you do something, it helps to retain it. My first lesson was pinning a pair of socks together. One reason—so the sock mate isn't lost—but more important was *where* you pinned them together. They are pinned at the toe so that if it causes a hole in one of the socks, they can still be worn because the hole won't be seen. If they are pinned at the top, it could break down the elastic, causing the sock top to fall down over the shoe—a look that would not be impressive at a job interview.

I learned that by having it explained to me. I never forgot it, even though it was **one time** over **seventeen years ago**. The lesson stuck!

Because the facility coordinators were gracious enough to show us around and wanted us to get a feel for how the place operated, we moved from one sector to another rather quickly. So, after what seemed like a very short time, I was promoted to a higher-level position. When it was announced that because of my "quick learning skills and eager attitude" I was being promoted to the coffee shop/book store, I received a rousing round of applause from my short-time co-workers. Hopefully, they explained to our co-workers that we were there on the fast-track from the start.

While I was going through my whirlwind training and moving from one assignment to another, Andy started out in the warehouse and was quickly promoted to the auto repair and body shop. Andy felt right at home—he already has a great deal of knowledge about working on cars, having kept our cars in tip top condition for over fifty-five years. At the time we were there, Delancey Street was servicing over five hundred vehicles ranging from clown cars for parades to eighteen-wheelers for moving and storage. All labor is done wearing rubber gloves at all times, because working there you're likely to get dirt or grease under your nails; and you may be serving dinner to the public at the five-star restaurant tonight. You can't have unsightly nails!

Which brings me to some of the services and business they operate that *totally support the facilities.*

I've already mentioned the five-star restaurant and the coffee shop/bookstore (which is also an art gallery). In addition, they have a catering company, as well as a wedding planning service.

At Christmas time, they have a tree lot and take it one step further by decorating many of the downtown business offices for the holiday season.

These Delancey Street businesses out-perform and out-service many of their competitors by providing more manpower and coming in under deadlines.

The complex houses a full-feature movie cinema company with cutting room. Movie stars are coming and going all day. A sixth Delancey-based home has recently been purchased in Massachusetts with the objective to train their residents in the arts.

All residents are required to learn at least three marketable skills while housed at Delancey.

During our short visit, we were blown away with the success of the operation. We found everyone very cordial and enthusiastic about how the place was run. Their success rate with rehabilitating "inmates" long-term soars in comparison with conventional Department of Corrections prisons.

How Are You Funded?

Through the Delancey Street Foundation, the six residential educational communities (REC's) function in identical fashion, both financially and operationally. The residents manage day-to-day procedures under the direction of Mimi Silbert and subject to oversight by a board of directors.

Typically, fifty-five to sixty-five percent of the operating funds come from pooling the resident-run training schools such as accounting, catering and moving; twenty-five to thirty-five percent of the funds come from products/services donations primarily from corporations; and about five to fifteen percent are provided by financial donations from individuals[*] and foundations. Their financial statements reflect ninety-nine percent of expenditures being allocated to programs, and less than one percent to administrative costs.

By contrast, in the DOC we currently have twenty-two prisons in Missouri alone. They house men and women in separate facilities. And the recidivism rate (re-entry into the prison system) is at seventy-five percent the last I heard.

---

[*] Please consider making a tax-deductible donation via their website: delancystreetfoundation.org

At Delancey, the sentences are shorter. They make a lot of their own food—actually they can *grow* their own food. Much healthier.

While MECC (the prison where Andy and I volunteer) does grow some food, it is donated to a shelter in the local area for the poor. While very benevolent, it does nothing to defray the cost of housing inmates.

Delancey residents work hard all day. Even though they have a workout room, nobody uses it because they are so tired that they just fall into bed at night! It's a *GOOD* tired.

For example, the dining hall used by everyone is stripped and re-waxed after every meal. Three times a day. Every day!

While at DOC, the hardest some of the offenders work is lifting weights. Most of their day is spent playing hand ball, walking the track, playing cards or dominoes, endlessly watching TV, napping, and/or shooting craps (until they get caught!).

Some men do work in maintenance, learn new job skills and have an opportunity to earn a small salary; but not enough job openings are available to go around and keep *all* of the eleven hundred men busy.

A portion of DOC population even takes classes, usually taught by volunteers. Occasionally, they may have to go to a mandated program. But that's a once-in-a-while case, and only available for certain offenders, depending on the crime.

And all the while they have to put up with security officers that aren't paid enough to cover their family's needs without both parents working, assuming there are two parents in the picture.

When I was a paid worker there, every custody employee, including the warden at that time, had a second job, and if he/she was married so did the spouse.

I suspect that if I had to work two jobs to support my family, I would be pretty tired and hard to live with. And if my husband had to also work two jobs, we wouldn't see much of each other—that wouldn't make me very happy either. Just food for thought . . .

Delancey Street website publishes their success rate at ninety-eight percent! Mostly, because when they walk out of there, they have a skill and *know they are somebody worthwhile*!

They have graduated over 14,000 men and women into society who are now leading successful lives. These grads include lawyers, truck drivers, salespeople, various medical professionals, realtors, mechanics, and contractors. Delancey alumni have found themselves such positions as a member of the San Francisco Board of Supervisors, President of the San Francisco Housing Commission, a Deputy Coroner, a fire department Captain, and a Deputy Sheriff.

I would be willing to bet that most of you reading this book have never heard of **Delancey Street Foundation**. But don't take my word for it, check it out for yourselves on the web at <u>delancystreetfoundation.org</u>. Google it to read what others have said! You will be amazed at what they learn and do there—and how they make it work.

And all of this at NO cost to the tax payer or the client!!!!!

Epilogue

I Can't Remember
2016 Until Now

In February 2016, Andy and I went in for our annual physicals with our young general practitioner who has since moved on to Des Moines, Iowa so that his wife could be closer to her family. We really liked him. I tried to talk him into moving her family down here to St. Louis, but apparently it wasn't in his budget. Anyway, he was going over our concerns regarding new issues or anything we might have questions about.

Andy made a casual comment that he had noticed me seeming to become more forgetful of late. I was under the impression that everybody forgets stuff now and then, and that I had been doing it for years. He insisted that it was more frequent than just "now and then" and was worried it might be something more serious. My argument was that I have always forgotten things—when you're trying to keep track of yourself, a husband and four kids, you're going to drop the ball every now and then.

As I was preparing to give him a good swift kick under the table, our doctor suggested, "Why don't we run a couple of tests, just to be cautious?"

The results of this series of tests confirmed my diagnosis. I did indeed have MCI (mild cognitive impairment), which is the general predecessor to Alzheimer's. The medical professionals involved in delivering this diagnosis did not have any treatment plan to prescribe. They suggested I investigate clinical studies to see if I could get accepted.

Very soon after this, an organization involved in a program that works with family issues having to do with memory loss came in to talk to a group of our St. Joseph's parishioners. Andy asked the man doing the program for a private conversation about me. The man told him to bring me in for some more cognitive testing.

It seems that this group was running a program with patients that were showing some decline in memory sharpness. This was being done in conjunction with a pharmaceutical company testing for an Alzheimer's study. If I met the criteria, all my medical expenses would be covered should I consent to be a case study.

Of course, their testing confirmed that I do, in fact, have the early stages of Alzheimer's, and I was accepted into the study. However, a year and a half year later, the study was closed due to lack of positive substantial results.

The fact that my condition was diagnosed early was instrumental, as we are discovering a myriad of research being done out there that may help me. It could be as simple as changing the way we eat. The old expression "We are what we eat" comes into play here big time. We've changed our diets to a much healthier menu. Whether or not it's helping the Alzheimer's is still up in the air, but the good news is that we've both lost weight and feel terrific.

I do want to share with you how I came to be able to give up driving due to this disease because I think you'll find it interesting.

Andy and I got involved with a support group through the Alzheimer's Association. We went to meetings that started with the patient and caregiver in the same session. Then after a break, we were separated from our caregivers so we would each share what we are learning as to how to deal with our circumstances. Or what new symptoms were showing up.

One week as we walked into the room, the coordinator asked, "How many of you are still driving?" Like most in the room, I raised my hand. A good number of us were still in the early stages. Then she proceeded to say that if any of us were to get into an accident, we could lose everything! She was very blunt and didn't pull any punches. She went on to tell us that with Alzheimer's, under duress our minds go blank.

She pointed out that in the case of any auto accident—those involved each tell their side of the incident, and both sides seldom match.

If the authorities ever find out that we are in an Alzheimer's program, study, or any related curriculum having to do with Alzheimer's, we lose **all** creditably. No matter how far along we are with the actual memory loss process, in times of stress, we just don't think clearly!

Many of the men in the group just poo-pooed her, saying, "They're not taking my license!" But, she got *my* attention!

After a few days, the fear factor began to wear off, and I decided to drive to meet my daughter for lunch.

I remember changing from one highway to another, and everything was going smoothly. It was a beautiful spring day. The sun was shining. All was well with my world. I even remember having the thought, *Everything is going so easily, I've got this! That instructor was just trying to employ a scare tactic!*

In less than ten minutes, I came up on a pack of cars sitting at a green light. When I realized that in SPITE of the green light they were NOT moving, I slammed on the brakes and killed the engine! I have a five on the floor stick shift and totally forgot to put my left foot on the clutch before bearing down on the brake pedal!

Fortunately, I came to a screeching halt before contacting another vehicle. But I couldn't get the car started after all the other cars cleared out. I kept turning the key and giving it gas, but nothing helped.

Instinctively, I remembered to say a quick, "Help me Jesus!" And the idea came immediately, *Call Andy*!

I'm looking in the rearview mirror, and cars are coming at me. Assuming that they were doing the speed limit at a swift forty-five miles per hour, I'm dead in the water.

As I'm calling Andy, a utility truck pulls up behind me and turns on his yellow flashing emergency light. This guy risks his own life to run interference for me. Then I hear Andy's voice on the phone and immediately feel comforted.

I tell him, "*I'm in trouble*!"

"Where are you?" he asks.

"North Highway 141 at Carmen Road."

Get this—he says, "*I'm coming up Carmen now—I'll be there in two minutes!*"

I hang up the phone. And a woman police officer is standing at my driver's side window! But because the car is dead, I can't lower the window, so I motion for her to come around to the passenger's side. It was also safer for her over there. I opened the passenger's side door from the inside. As I start to explain the dilemma, another guy sticks his head in the opened passenger side door, and in a firm voice says, "*Turn OFF the ignition*!! *Now start it up. Okay, pull over to the side.*" By the time Andy got there, I was safely parked out of harm's way, and traffic had resumed. Is God fast, or what!?

After the initial shock from this incident wore off, I knew that God was holding me in the palm of His hand. And no matter what the outcome, I'm going to be good! Or, as a dear friend who passed away from cancer used to say all the time, "Either way, I win!"

That was the last time I drove. Footnote—we were able to sell the car to a single dad with four or five teenage boys. The make and model were exactly what he was looking for.

You've Got To Believe

I knew soon after I received my initial diagnosis that I wanted to write this book. Part of it was because I wanted to preserve my memories while I could still access them. But the biggest motivation was that I honestly feel I had a story to tell—an experience to share—an inspiration that might hit home with someone searching for their purpose or a deeper meaning to life.

The work on the manuscript came much more easily than I would have imagined. God took charge, and I literally couldn't wait to get out of bed in the morning to get to my computer. You are holding the results of the five months' efforts in your hands, and I hope these words have touched you in some small (or maybe a very large) way.

I do know this—the project has been incredibly fulfilling. It has given me purpose and direction. And in spite of the Alzheimer's diagnosis, I have an utter sense of peace about it all. Taking it one day at a time with my best friend and life partner by my side, I will get through this journey and soak up whatever lessons God has in store for me.

Just at the point I was trying to figure out a title for this book, God put it in front of me in the form of a vanity license plate I happened to notice. It said UGT2BLV. I immediately recognized God's message to me—and indeed the entire backbone of the course of my life.

YOU'VE GOT TO BELIEVE!

Make this your mantra. Drive it into your brain. Don't ever forget that God's got your back, ***no matter what.***

Take the good with the bad and watch like a hawk for your opportunities to grow spiritually. They are right in front of your nose if you will only open your heart and let the lessons take hold.

If you enjoyed this book and would like to contact the author, she would love to hear from you. You can reach her at: UGT2BLV@gmail.com.